DICK & PAT —

It HAS BEEN A
PLEASURE to WORK WITH
YOU OVER THE YEARS to HELP
ACHIEVE YOUR FINANCIAL
Best wishes on LIVIN
MEANINGFUL AND ABUNDANT LIFE

Jim Howard

FEBRUARY 2012

THE
WEALTH
SOLUTION

Bringing Structure to Your Financial Life

Steven Atkinson, Joni Clark, Eric Golberg & Alex Potts

Afterword by DR. HARRY M. MARKOWITZ,
Recipient of the Nobel Prize in Economic Sciences

IRN: R 10-239

First edition

Printed in China

Library of Congress Control Number: 2011920405

ISBN: 978-0-615-43722-4

For his friendship, his courage and his passion

for empowering investors through education,

this book is dedicated to the memory of

Gordon Murray.

Foreword

Would you rather be rich or wealthy? I believe there is a difference. To me, being rich means having a lot of money, living extravagantly and accumulating all the latest material things. On the other hand, being wealthy is about living an abundant life. Being wealthy is so much more than just having a lot of money. It's about setting meaningful goals for yourself and your family and then making smart financial decisions to achieve those goals. Being wealthy is a long-term lifestyle, one that spans generations.

If you are more interested in being wealthy than being rich, then *The Wealth Solution* can guide you along the path to success. The concepts within this book provide insights into how today's wealthy families create, enhance and sustain their wealth over time. This structured process has been the foundation that has enabled individuals and families lead lives that are both highly satisfying and deeply meaningful.

How do I know that this approach works? The answer is simple: I use it every day to help my clients achieve their most important goals and dreams.

In more than 30 years in the financial services industry, I have learned what creates success for affluent families. I have observed that it takes a lot of financial discipline to plan, save and invest for the future. You have to be willing to live on 70%-80% of your net income—not 100%-110%.

My goal from day one has been to make a difference in people's lives and do what I could to get them to a secure and comfortable financial future. I remember when I was looking into a career as a financial advisor way back as a college freshman. I was given a study by a friend in the industry showing that out of 100 25-year-olds, 54 would likely be dependent on family, friends, charities or others at age 65. Worse, only five of the 100 would be considered wealthy at that age and would achieve the retirements they wanted for themselves. Those numbers shocked me. I said to myself, "Maybe I can do something to help others gain financial independence."

My parents had an enormous impact on what I do and how I do it. My father was a true entrepreneur: He did well through real estate developing and various small businesses, and he even sold some patents for his inventions. He showed me early on that being confident in your abilities, taking smart risks and working hard pays off. His example really inspired me to get my investment and insurance licenses and start practicing financial planning while I was still in college. Then, when graduation came and I was getting job offers from some of the largest firms at the time, I opted to be my own boss and start my own practice in San Jose. I was 24 years old and I knew no one in the area. But with some confidence, a willingness to take smart risks and a lot of hard work, I built my one-man shop into a successful business. Since those humble beginnings, I have had the opportunity to work for some of the largest financial services firms in the country and have now come full circle, working today as the owner and managing principal of an independent wealth management firm.

Values my parents taught me guide me to this day as a husband and father and also in my involvement with Boy Scouts and other youth groups. And of course, they also guide me as a wealth manager to my clients. A great wealth manager does his best to inspire people to make smart choices as early as possible that allow them to achieve meaningful, long-term financial success. There's a great quote that I'm very fond of: *The battles are won in the general's tent long before the battle is joined.* You need a plan if you want to succeed. Without that plan, you probably won't make it. And more than anything, I want to see my clients achieve success.

Structured Wealth Management clearly illustrates the strategy for success that I learned many years ago. I got frustrated trying to pick winning investments for my clients. It seemed that the winners one year often turned out to be the losers the very next year. But when I discovered the academic research that is the basis for this approach, it was like a light bulb went on. Instead of spending all my time trying to outguess the market, I could instead help my clients focus on what really counts—setting meaningful life goals and then positioning their wealth to get them to those goals on time and with as little stress as possible. The *Structured Wealth Management* approach showed me that you're not a great investor (or a great advisor) if you pick the best funds—you're great if you build and maintain a plan that allows you to achieve the life you want for you and your family.

In fact, I believe that we owe it to ourselves and the world around us to make the smartest possible choices about our wealth. As Americans, we are truly blessed—a fact that I was starkly reminded of during a trip with my family to Africa. There we visited several schools and saw how much they lack in the basics that we all take for granted. To be born in America and to have all that we possess means that we have a responsibility to help others. We owe it to the people we care about and the people who need our help to be good stewards of our wealth so that it can create many beneficial opportunities in the world. You can be reckless and squander that opportunity, or you can plan intelligently so you can share, give and help yourself and others.

I invite you to read on and learn how you can take the right steps to achieving a higher level of financial success and then use that wealth to build a truly abundant, truly wealthy life.

— RONALD J. HOWARD
Managing Principal
Siena Wealth Management, Inc.

Table of Contents

Chapter 1
A Framework for Financial Success 1

Chapter 2
The Key Challenges Facing Today's Investors 7

Chapter 3
The *Structured Wealth Management* Solution............ 15

Chapter 4
The Investment Planning Process: An Overview 25

Chapter 5
Markets Work 29

Chapter 6
Risk & Return Are Related 51

Chapter 7
Diversify with Structure..65

Chapter 8
Building and Implementing Your Investment Portfolio............ 83

Chapter 9
Invest for the Long Term 93

Chapter 10
Advanced Planning and Trusted Advisory Relationships.......... 107

Chapter 11
Putting It All Together 121

Chapter 12
Selecting the Right Advisor....................................... 129

Afterword 141

About the Authors.. 143

Acknowledgements 147

CHAPTER 1

A Framework for Financial Success

"Being rich is having money; being wealthy is having time."
— Henry Ward Beecher

A few years ago, a friend who worked as an executive at a huge technology firm in Silicon Valley found herself in a dismal financial situation — facing an enormous tax bill on stock option gains that, for a variety of reasons, never found their way to her bottom line. Suddenly, instead of enjoying a well-earned retirement, replete with sunny vacations to exotic places and free time to spend with friends and family — she was forced to continue working for many more years in order to help rebuild the wealth that she never should have lost in the first place.

Her story is troubling and all too common, even for sophisticated, educated investors. We've seen too many similar financial missteps over the years. Too many investors never reach their most important goals — not because they aren't smart or don't make the effort, but because they don't use a successful plan to help them get there. As a result, they end up compromising not just their own futures, but the futures of their families.

Our goal is to give you the tools you need to make smarter financial decisions — and avoid the mistakes that too often trip up investors. We are committed to making sure that investors have everything they need to achieve all that is important to them and their loved ones.

If you're like the vast majority of investors today, you could use such tools and guidance. Saving and investing to reach your financial goals can often seem like a huge challenge. And chances are, you're at least a little uncertain about whether the decisions you're making with your money in a variety of key areas — from investing for retirement to minimizing taxes to paying for a child's college tuition — are the right decisions.

You are the reason why we've written this book. It will give you an actionable framework to help you make better, wiser, more informed decisions in all areas of your financial life.

To get started, we need to acknowledge an important fact. It's become harder than ever to navigate through the increasing complexity of our financial lives and ensure that we are making consistently smart moves with our money. Achieving major financial goals was challenging enough even before the so-called "Great Recession" and the tremendous upheaval in the financial markets in recent years. In the wake of those historic events, many investors feel more confused and uncertain about their futures and how to get back on the right track.

When we first sat down together to discuss the idea of writing a book to help investors, it was in late December 2009 — the tail end of a decade that saw the worst 10-year return for the Dow Jones Industrial Average since the 1930s. During that time, many investors watched their hard-earned savings plummet in value. Many questioned their approach to saving, spending and investing, and worried that they would have to delay or forgo some of their key life objectives such as a comfortable retirement, or leaving a legacy to their children. This fear that many investors experienced during the worst of the recent downturn is not easily forgotten — and has left many wondering how to get back on track and stay there over the long run.

But if that's the reality today, it's important to recognize another fact: There is a process that can enable you to cut through all the confusion and noise, simplify your financial life and help ensure that you're making the smartest possible decisions about your money consistently — day in and day out. What's more, it's a prudent, time-tested process based on empirical evidence about how the financial markets operate, a process used by some of the most successful families in America to manage their wealth.

This process — called *Structured Wealth Management* — is what this book is all about. As you'll discover, *Structured Wealth Management* is a fundamentally different method for managing your financial life from those used by other investors (including most financial advisors and investment professionals). It is designed to help you solve your biggest financial issues — including investments, taxes, estate planning, wealth preservation and protection, and charitable giving.

Structured Wealth Management: An Overview

Structured Wealth Management is a defined and disciplined process that consists of a number of closely connected steps. We'll explore this process in greater detail in the following chapters. For now, it's helpful to understand three main characteristics:

- *Structured Wealth Management* is consultative. *Structured Wealth Management* helps you identify and clarify the specific financial goals that are truly important to you — those that hold the most meaning and will have the greatest impact for you and your loved ones. By beginning with this step, all your future financial decisions can be made "with a purpose" — that is, within the context of your key objectives. This method is distinctly different from other approaches, in that it steers you to make decisions based not on events in the markets or the economy but on the steps you should take to further your progress toward your unique goals.

Wealth management should not be concerned with picking hot stocks or trying to beat the overall market. Instead, wealth management blocks out the "noise" by encouraging investors to answer an extremely powerful question: What should I be doing with my money to provide the life I want most?

This approach to wealth management tangibly puts tremendous purpose behind your financial decisions. Your timeframe and perspective are immeasurably broadened, and you no longer have to worry about what the stock market is doing today or this month or even this year. You are no longer thinking tactically, but strategically. Your plan is based around a desired long-term outcome — not on beating the market or simply guarding your wealth from short-term losses.

- ***Structured Wealth Management* is comprehensive.** Many investors focus only on one aspect of their financial lives — often their investment portfolios or 401(k) accounts. Of course, smart investment choices are crucial to achieving long-term financial goals such as a secure retirement. But for nearly all of us, there are other vital issues that need to be addressed to make our goals come to fruition. Depending on your circumstances, these needs could range from saving for future college tuition costs to helping aging parents meet health care needs to providing for children and heirs to supporting your favorite non-profit organizations and causes.

Unlike many approaches to financial planning, wealth management addresses the full range of financial-related issues that investors and their families face. What's more, it ties all those various pieces and moving parts together seamlessly, so that the components of your financial life — investments, insurance, wills and trusts and so on — always work together as effectively as possible to achieve the meaningful goals you've set.

- *Structured Wealth Management* **is rooted in facts, data and analysis.**
Based on decades of financial data and research, this rational and
practical approach helps investors avoid making rash, emotional
decisions that could derail their plans and make it harder for them
to reach their goals. For example, many investors in the wake of
the financial crisis of 2008 and 2009 became fearful of investing in
the financial markets. But we know from history that markets have
tended to work in the long run — despite the occasional crisis.

In order to fully take advantage of *Structured Wealth Management*
and make the most of its benefits, we encourage you to work in
partnership with a financial advisor who uses the type of approach
we outline in this book.

The reason is simple: Successfully managing all the key aspects of your
financial life is a complex process — one that can require a great deal
of time and attention to detail to get right. In our experience, we've
seen that most investors lack the time, knowledge or desire needed
to manage their wealth. As a result, we have found that investors
tend to end up in much stronger financial shape when they enlist
a professional whose job is to stay acutely focused on their clients'
financial lives and the *Structured Wealth Management* process at all
times. This is not to say that it is impossible to implement *Structured
Wealth Management* on your own and have a better financial life.

But this process will be so time consuming and requires such extensive
knowledge and specialization, it is not very practical for the majority
of investors. We believe it makes sense for your wealth management
efforts to be as successful as they possibly can — and that working
in partnership with the right kind of financial advisor offers a much
surer and smoother path to achieving your financial goals.

Why You Need *Structured Wealth Management*

The term "wealth management" may seem a little off-putting if you don't think of yourself as particularly wealthy. The truth is, you don't have to be among the super-rich to make the wealth management process a successful and important part of your financial life. Quite the contrary. We all face numerous financial goals, challenges and choices, from paying for today's bills to funding goals that might be decades away to leaving a lasting legacy. These concerns won't solve themselves or go away if you ignore them. Indeed, by disregarding them, you're simply asking for someone else to make the decisions about how and where your money is used.

If you don't want to be dependent on or beholden to others, you need to effectively manage the money you do have. Wealth management's aim is to help you make smart, rational choices about your finances so that you can control your own destiny and build the life you want for yourself and your family. This approach makes wealth management entirely applicable to your life — regardless of whether you have $100,000 or $20 million. It is designed to help address issues that almost all of us will have to face at some point in our lives. So ask yourself: Do you want to create a plan to address those issues structurally, or do you want to leave it all to chance?

We think the answer is obvious. You have an obligation to make wise choices about your wealth and do all you can to avoid frittering it away. The reason: Your wealth can create a world of good — for yourself, your spouse, your children, grandchildren, and beyond. So whether or not you "feel" wealthy isn't the point. In the end, your assets can be a tremendously positive force in many, many lives. But you have to take proper care of them to make all that happen.

We'd like to show you how.

CHAPTER 2

The Key Challenges Facing Today's Investors

To understand how *Structured Wealth Management* may help you achieve financial success, it's necessary to first recognize the most significant issues affecting investors today.

Chances are you're finding it more challenging than ever these days to wrap your arms around your increasingly complex financial life and make good sense of the entire picture. But the sooner you determine where you are now and where you want to be in the future, the sooner you can set out to build a plan that tackles the major issues that impact your life.

For more than two decades, we have worked closely with hundreds of top financial advisors who together serve thousands of investors. Our experience helping advisors help their clients achieve their most important financial goals has taught us that investors today share six major concerns:

Concern 1: Preserving Wealth in Retirement

How are you going to grow and preserve your wealth so that you have the money required to meet your needs and fulfill your goals — not just today, but for decades to come?

It's a huge question — one that investors are asking themselves more and more. The vast majority, regardless of their level of wealth, are concerned about preserving their wealth so they will have enough money throughout retirement.

This makes perfect sense. Few of us want to be forced to downsize our lifestyles. And yet, many investors are not financially positioned to maximize their chances of maintaining their lifestyles during retirement — especially when you consider the challenges that today's pre-retirees and retirees must contend with. For example:

- **Inflation's impact.** Rising prices can decimate your purchasing power, savings and your ability to preserve wealth throughout your golden years. Assuming the long-term historical annual inflation rate of around 3%, an annual fixed income of $100,000 would be worth just $86,000 in five years and only about $40,000 in 30 years. The same purchase that would cost $100,000 today would soar to more than $240,000 in 30 years. And if inflation runs at a much higher rate than normal for an extended period — a real concern given the huge amount of government spending that has occurred in recent years — the goal of wealth preservation and income replacement throughout retirement could become even tougher to achieve.

- **Rising life expectancies.** Thanks to continued advances in health care, American seniors are living 50 percent longer than they were in the 1930s. According to the Centers for Disease Control, a 65-year-old can now expect to live another 18 years, on average.[1] For a 65-year-old married couple, there's a 58% chance that one of them will live to 90 and a 29% chance that one will reach 95.[2] While that is certainly good news, it also means that you must make your money last much longer or risk running out of money before you die.

- **Soaring health care costs.** The cost of health care has been rising at a much faster pace than the overall rate of inflation in recent years. This should be of particular concern to aging investors who are more likely than younger Americans to consume substantial amounts of health care goods and services. What's more, Medicare might only cover about 50% of a typical retiree's medical expenses. Consider that seniors age 65 and over spend an average of $4,888 per person annually for deductibles, copayments, premiums and other health care costs not covered by insurance, according to the most recent National Health Expenditure Survey.[3] That amount is more than two times the amount spent by average non-elderly adults. And the largest expenditures occurred among those 85 and older. According to the Employee Benefit Research Institute (EBRI), a retired couple age 65 would need approximately $338,000 to have a 90% chance of covering their out-of-pocket health care expenses in retirement.[4]

- **A weakened Social Security system.** It's no secret that Social Security has long been in trouble, but a look at the numbers is particularly sobering. Under current assumptions, Social Security trust fund expenses are expected to exceed income from taxes some time around 2016. By 2024, those expenses are expected to exceed income from taxes plus interest income, and the trust fund is expected to be exhausted by 2037, according to EBRI.[5]

- **The diminished role of pensions.** Retirement has become a largely self-funded venture, as evidenced by the fact that just 32% of workers today participate in some type of defined benefit (pension) plan. That's down from a full 84% in 1980, according to EBRI. These days, the majority of workers (55%) participate in defined contribution plans — 401(k)s and the like.[6]

- **Taking care of kids and parents.** According to the Pew Research Center, one out of every eight Americans, ages 40 to 60, is raising a child while also caring for at least one aged parent at home. In addition, roughly 7 to 10 million Americans are caring for their aging parents from a long distance away.[7]

---

1 Center for Disease Control and Prevention, "National Vital Statistics Reports," Vol. 56, No. 10, 2008

2 American Academy of Actuaries, 2008.

3 "National Health Expenditure Data: Personal Health Care Spending by Age Group and Source Of Payment, Calendar Year 2004," Centers for Medicare and Medicaid Services

4 "Savings Needed for Health Expenses in Retirement: An Examination of Persons Ages 55 and 65 in 2009," June 2009, Vol. 30, No. 6, Employee Benefit Research Institute, 2009

5 "The Basics of Social Security Updated with the 2009 Board of Trustees Report," July 2009, Employee Benefit Research Institute

6 EBRI Databook on Employee Benefits, updated April 2010, Employee Benefits Research Institute

7 "From The Age of Aquarius to the Age of Responsibility," Pew Research Center, 2005.

The end result: Too many investors saving for retirement today face a higher level of uncertainty about their future prospects than their parents and grandparents did. In the wake of that uncertainty, you simply have to be smarter, plan better and question many of the assumptions long-held by previous generations and many in the financial services industry. We believe that traditional "rules of thumb" advice such as needing 70% of your working income during retirement cannot be taken as gospel anymore. Your retirement plan needs to reflect the realities of the world today and going forward. In chapters five through nine, we will explore how you can position your portfolio to capture the growth and profits that the financial markets generate, while minimizing downside risk through proper portfolio allocation and ongoing risk maintenance and rebalancing.

Concern 2: Minimizing Taxes

You've probably heard the adage that "it's not what you make, it's what you keep that counts." Not surprisingly, mitigating income taxes is a major concern for most investors. No one enjoys paying taxes and income taxes are typically the most obvious and onerous taxes investors face. In addition, mitigating estate taxes and capital gains taxes also ranks high on the list of many investors' concerns.

Such concerns are well founded, as taxes can significantly erode your ability to grow and preserve wealth. From 1926 through 2009, for example, stocks as represented by the S&P 500 Index, gained 9.8% annually. After taxes, however, that return fell to just 7.7%. Bonds' 5.4% annual return dropped to a mere 3.4% once taxes were taken into account. In real terms, a $1 investment in stocks back in 1926 would have grown, before taxes, to $2,592 at the end of 2009 — but just $510 on an after-tax basis.[8]

There's cause for additional concern. Taxes during the past decade or so have been hovering at relatively low levels — but may be set to rise. Trying to predict tax code changes is a risky bet, of course. But you need to be aware that higher taxes across the board could be on their way — and at the very least, build flexibility into your plan so you can make adjustments should your tax situation change. The good news: You can take steps to minimize the taxes you pay and keep more of what is yours by using a variety of wealth management techniques, such as tax efficient investment vehicles and smart asset location strategies that will be explored later.

Concern 3: Effective Estate and Gift Transfer

The ancient Chinese adage that "wealth never survives three generations" seems equally applicable today. A major concern for many investors is ensuring that their heirs, parents, children and grandchildren are well provided for in accordance with their wishes. And yet, our experience is that most investors don't have an estate plan — and many of those who do, have outdated plans. Even more troubling: 65% of all American adults don't even have a will, according to a 2009 Harris Interactive study.[9]

Many investors don't take the appropriate actions in this key area of their financial lives because they assume they don't possess enough wealth to necessitate an estate plan. Regardless of your net worth, the ability to ensure that your assets go to where you want them to has numerous and important potential implications — from being able to help a child or grandchild go to college to ensuring the continuity of a family-owned business to simply avoiding probate. Take college tuition, for example. College education expenses have risen at a rate of more than 5% annually during the past decade, according to the College Board.[10] That means a child born today could need over $220,000 to attend a four-year public college in 2028 — more than triple today's college costs.

Passing on wealth and using it to benefit your heirs as you see fit doesn't happen automatically — it requires the implementation of the right strategies for your goals and situation. As you'll see later, those strategies might include everything from correct titling of assets to smart gifting strategies and trusts designed to provide maximum benefits to a spouse, family members or charities.

8 Morningstar, Inc. 2010

9 www.lawyers.com/understand-your-legal-issue/press-room/2010-Will-Survey-Press-Release.html

10 "Trends in College Pricing 2009," The College Board

Concern 4: Wealth and Income Protection

A significant number of investors today are worried about keeping wealth safe from potential creditors, litigants, children's spouses and potential ex-spouses, as well as from catastrophic loss. They also want to be sure that their loved ones are protected in the wake of major health problems or other unforeseen events. Certainly many professionals (such as attorneys and physicians), business owners and entrepreneurs need to focus on protecting their hard-earned wealth. And in today's highly litigious culture, nearly everyone needs to consider the possibility of having their wealth unjustly taken from them. Increasingly, investors are realizing the importance of confronting some tough and potentially uncomfortable questions:

• What would happen if I was the victim of a frivolous lawsuit?

• What would happen if one of my children married a "gold digger," then divorced and was sued for a large sum?

• What would happen if one of my children was in an accident in my car or someone suffered an injury in my home?

• What if a major disability prevented me from working and generating an income for my family?

• What if I end up needing to live in a nursing home or require home health care services?

Wealth management strategies aimed at wealth protection can motivate creditors to settle, mitigate the possibility of being sued or minimize the financial impact of a judgment. Various trusts and business structures can work effectively in this area. Trusts and insurance can also play a role in protecting your wealth and income from an unexpected hardship. We'll examine some of these strategies in Chapter 10.

Concern 5: Charitable Gifting

Helping to facilitate and increase the effectiveness of their charitable intentions is also very important to many investors. From direct gifts to formal gifting structures like donor advised funds and private family foundations, many investors are looking to ensure that their money is being used by their chosen charities to generate the maximum impact on the social and economic issues they care about most.

Simultaneously, these investors want to make sure that their philanthropic goals don't conflict with or endanger their own financial futures and their ability to secure a comfortable retirement for themselves and leave a legacy for their families.

Concern 6: Finding High-Quality Financial Advice

Many investors have long been concerned about working with capable financial professionals. It's little wonder. For decades, much of the financial services industry has been driven by a sales-oriented culture that stressed pushing products instead of providing comprehensive wealth management services.

This concern reached a peak during the market downturn of 2008 and 2009 fueled by enormous market volatility, the revelation of the largest Ponzi scheme in history, and the fact that the largest investment firms in the world suffered tremendous losses from bad investment decisions they made on their own behalf. All of this created a significant and still-growing sense of dissatisfaction in and distrust of the financial services industry among many investors. Consider the following from a 2008 Survey:

- 81 percent of investors said that they planned to take money away from their current advisor.

- 86 percent of investors planned to tell other investors to avoid their advisor.

- A mere 2 percent planned to recommend their advisor to other investors.[11]

We recognize that many of you are looking for guidance and assistance in managing your financial life. With that in mind, we've included a chapter in this book to help you find professionals who offer objective advice and who would act as a true fiduciary on your behalf. The good news is that during the past decade or so, more and more advisors have begun implementing a true wealth management process and acting as

11 Prince and Associates, 2008

fiduciaries to their clients. If you choose to work with an advisor, you may find great benefit in using the guidelines and best practices in this book.

You most likely share at least some or possibly all of the aforementioned financial concerns. Each one is a sizable challenge on its own — and taken together, they present you with a potentially enormous hurdle on your path to a comfortable, secure and meaningful financial life. This is where the wealth management process brings tremendous value. By helping you develop integrated solutions to these concerns and creating a plan that strikes the optimal balance between them, you can simplify your financial picture and achieve greater overall financial success than you could by dealing with these challenges on a case-by-case basis.

CHAPTER 3

The *Structured Wealth Management* Solution

As you've seen, the financial challenges you face may be sizable and complex — and they can affect every facet of your life. To address them, you need a disciplined process that will allow you to consistently make the prudent decisions that will help you achieve your most important goals. Without this approach, you may needlessly put your future and your family's future at risk.

We believe that the most effective way for most investors to address the many challenges they face is by adopting a comprehensive *Structured Wealth Management* process. Indeed, that's exactly what many of today's most successful families are doing.

But what exactly do we mean by comprehensive *Structured Wealth Management*? The term "wealth management" has become a buzzword in recent years. Financial advisors of all types are now calling themselves "wealth managers" and claiming to offer wealth management services. Unfortunately, many of these advisors are wealth managers in name only — after all, the title "wealth manager" sounds much more impressive than "stockbroker."

We believe that wealth management is not a term open to interpretation or multiple definitions. In order to benefit from true wealth management, you need to make sure you're actually bringing together wealth management professionals who possess the capabilities and expertise to address your biggest financial challenges and goals.

Structured Wealth Management Defined

At its core, *Structured Wealth Management* encompasses each specific area of your financial life (i.e. tax planning, estate planning, risk management, etc.) employing professionals who have expertise in these specific areas.

The wealth management process stands in stark contrast to how most investors operate today. The vast majority of investors tend to address financial goals like college and estate planning on an ad hoc basis — treating these issues as separate concerns. These investors neglect to understand that the complex scope of issues they face are often deeply interconnected and must be managed in a coordinated manner. Usually, issues are dealt with only as they arise, and typically just enough information is gathered to implement the particular solution to the problem at hand.

Structured Wealth Management should be thought of as a detailed blueprint guiding all your decisions, ensuring that they all work together in a coordinated manner.

Structured Wealth Management accomplishes this in three ways:

1. **Using a consultative process** to gain a detailed understanding of your deepest values and goals. This process helps ensure that your wealth is utilized to pursue your key life objectives.

2. **Employing customized solutions designed to fit your specific needs and goals beyond simply investments.** The range of services and tools involved in crafting wealth management solutions might include insurance, estate planning, business planning and retirement planning.

3. **Delivering these customized solutions in close consultation with other professional advisors.** This enables investors to work closely — and in a coordinated manner — with trusted advisors to identify potential issues, implement solutions and regularly monitor your overall financial situation. Such advisors offer valuable expertise, perspectives and analysis that can help investors avoid making irrational decisions that jeopardize their financial goals.

Broadly, this process incorporates all the main components of wealth management:

- **Investment planning** allocates your assets based on goals, return objectives, time horizons and risk tolerance and is the foundation upon which a comprehensive wealth management solution is created.

- **Advanced planning** addresses the entire range of financial needs beyond investments in four primary areas: wealth enhancement, wealth transfer, wealth protection and charitable gifting.

- **Trusted advisory relationships** are created by assembling and managing a network of experts who will be involved in providing solutions to a variety of financial issues where they have specialized expertise.

To organize your thinking and approach to wealth management, you can use this formula:

Structured Wealth Management = **investment planning + advanced planning + trusted advisory relationships**

Investors rarely take this type of coordinated and comprehensive approach with their finances. This can lead to problems that may jeopardize the financial health of their families, their businesses and themselves. This is why wealth management is so important: It enables you to see the big picture at all times and make decisions within this framework instead of focusing on only one aspect.

Incorporating a *Structured Wealth Management* approach requires you to think through the full range of the financial challenges you and your family face, and develop optimal solutions that work in a coordinated manner. Whether you act as your own wealth manager or work collaboratively with a professional wealth advisor, you will gain a tremendous advantage over other investors who take a less disciplined, ad hoc approach to managing their financial lives.

The Wealth Management Consultative Process

The Wealth Management Consultative Process is a formal series of five structured steps, which are typically conducted as meetings:

1. **The Discovery Meeting.** This first step is to help you uncover and clearly identify your true financial goals — the things you want and need most out of life. The overarching goal of the Discovery Meeting is to understand your unique situation — your key goals and values — and identify the challenges you face in achieving what is most important to you. Once these goals are established and understood, your optimal plan can be designed.

2. **The Investment Plan Meeting.** At this meeting, the wealth manager presents a detailed series of investment recommendations designed around the information uncovered during the Discovery Meeting.

   A well-crafted investment plan can help ensure that your investment decisions are based on rational analysis, which can help you avoid making long-term investment decisions based on emotional responses to short-term or one-time events. Each investment plan should include these seven important areas of discussion:

   - **Your long-term goals, objectives and values.** Long-term goals can consist of anything from early retirement to purchasing a new home to achieving financial independence. These goals are the bedrock upon which your investment plan will be based.

   - **The expected time horizon for your investments.** Your time horizon consists of the period of time your portfolio is expected to remain invested. For example, a 65 year old retiree should plan for a potential time horizon of at least 25 to 30 years.

   - **A definition of the level of risk that you are willing and able to accept.** It is important for you to understand the amount of risk you are willing and able to tolerate during your investment time horizon. In designing your portfolio, your advisor will help you determine both your financial risk tolerance (the amount of loss you might have to absorb in order to meet your goals) and your emotional risk tolerance as well (the amount of loss that you can accept without acting on your emotions by changing your predetermined asset allocation).

- **The rate-of-return objective and asset classes that will be used.** Your advisor will help to identify the specific return/risk profiles of each potential portfolio, and use these profiles as the framework to determine your asset allocation.

- **The investment methodology that will be used.** We firmly believe that investors are best served by accepting a market rate of return and using low-cost investment vehicles in order to try and achieve that return.

- **A rebalancing plan.** You also will need to establish the means for rebalancing and making periodic adjustments to the portfolio as needed. Rebalancing your portfolio will help ensure it maintains the desired risk and return parameters.

- **Monitoring and reporting methods.** Your goals won't remain static over time — they'll change as your life changes. That's why it's important to regularly monitor your portfolio and ensure it reflects where you are today and where you want to be down the road.

3. **The Mutual Commitment Meeting.** It's important that you consider the proposed investment plan thoroughly before committing to work with a wealth manager. After you have reviewed the plan carefully, this meeting will allow you to ask any questions or voice concerns you have about the plan and decide whether to move ahead with implementation.

4. **The 45-Day Follow-up Meeting.** This meeting allows your wealth manager to help you understand and organize the financial documentation involved in working together. It's also an opportunity to review any initial concerns and questions.

5. **Regular Progress Meetings**. Regular Progress Meetings focus on reviewing the steps you've taken toward meeting your various goals and making any necessary adjustments based on changes in your personal, professional or financial situation.

The Discovery Meeting and Total Investor Profile

As noted above, one reason why wealth management can be so effective in addressing investors' needs is because of the Discovery Meeting, which is focused on helping you identify your most important financial goals. The reality is, you simply cannot solve the complex and sometimes conflicting issues you face until you position your financial assets around the values, needs, goals and issues that are most significant to you.

The Discovery Meeting enables you to identify all that is truly important to you in seven key areas of your life. In working with an advisor, there must be a close and thorough understanding between you in these seven areas — an understanding that goes well beyond the simplistic aspects of a typical investment review. Your answers to the types of questions below will enable you to develop a holistic, all-encompassing picture of your life goals so that your assets can be positioned appropriately:

1. **Values.** What is truly important to you about your money and your desire for success, and what are the key, deep-seated values underlying the decisions you make to attain them? When you think about your money, what concerns, needs or feelings come to mind?

2. **Goals.** What do you want to achieve with your money over the long run — professionally and personally, practically and ideally?

3. **Relationships.** Who are all the people in your life who are important to you — including family, employees, friends, perhaps even pets?

4. **Assets.** What do you own — from your business to real estate to investment accounts and retirement plans — and where and how are your assets held? Conversely, what do you owe to lenders, and what continuing obligations do you have (to family, charities, etc.)?

5. **Advisors.** Whom do you rely upon for advice, and how do you feel about the professional relationships you currently have?

6. **Process.** How actively do you like to be involved in managing your financial life, and how do you prefer to work with your trusted advisors?

7. **Interests.** What are your passions in life — including your hobbies, sports and leisure activities, charitable and philanthropic involvements, religious and spiritual proclivities, and children's schools and activities?

If you have a spouse or partner, he or she should be equally involved in this discussion. It's not uncommon for couples to have differing values, priorities or interests. Such differences need to be recognized and accounted for so that you have a better understanding and appreciation of each other — and so that the plan you create can be effective in meeting your collective goals.

Your wealth manager can then use that information to create a Total Investor Profile that will serve as a roadmap — a guide so that every financial decision you make supports what you want most from life (see Exhibit 3.1).

If, like many investors, you currently work with one or more financial advisors, you are probably aware that most use some type of fact-finding process in the first meeting. However, you may also have noticed that these questions usually focus entirely on your investable assets and net worth. In contrast, note that only one of the seven categories that make up wealth management's Total Investor Profile concerns assets. Six of the seven are focused on helping you (and your wealth manager) better understand who you are as a person. By engaging in this Discovery Process and using the insights learned from it to create a personalized profile, your wealth and all the choices you make about it become perfectly aligned with the life you want to build for yourself, your family and those you care about most.

Exhibit 3.1: The Total Investor Profile

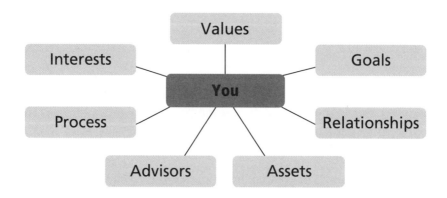

Of the seven categories that make up the Total Investor Profile, we believe the most important is the one representing your values.

Values are one of the core motivations for everything we do in our lives, and have a profound impact on every important decision we make, from what we choose to do for a living to whom we marry to how we spend our free time — in short, who we are as people. For example, if you're a parent you probably value your children above almost everything else in the world. As a result, you want to protect them, to educate them well and to set them onto a smooth path in life. Financially speaking, one of the things you may want to do is build an adequate college fund for your children's education. This is a common goal. But underlying that goal is the fundamental value of loving your children. Values run the gamut from the basic — such as security, financial freedom and not having to worry about paying the bills — to deeper such as family, community, faith and reasons for being.

As important as values are, however, most of us are not particularly good at articulating them. The Discovery Meeting step can therefore bring substantial advantages to the process of managing wealth effectively by helping you uncover and clarify your core values.

One way to go about this is to ask yourself: "What is important to me about money?"

Let's say that your first answer is "Security." You would then want to ask yourself, "Well, what is so important to me about security?" You might decide that the answer is "Knowing that I can take care of my family." You would then ask, "What is important to me about taking care of my family?" You would continue uncovering your values in this way until there is nothing more important to you than the last value you stated. At that point, you will have uncovered your single most important value.

While this is straightforward on the surface, it's important to realize that it takes perseverance to drill down to your most important value. Most of us simply don't spend a lot of time thinking about the issue. That is why the best results occur by having a collaborative conversation about values with an advisor.

In the following chapters, we'll explore each of the three main components of wealth management — investment planning, advanced planning and trusted advisory relationships — in more detail. Armed with this information, you'll be ideally positioned to bring solutions to your financial issues and achieve your biggest goals.

CHAPTER 4

The Investment Planning Process: An Overview

Investment planning is the foundation of a properly *Structured Wealth Management* plan. While not everyone needs to worry about minimizing estate taxes or effective charitable giving strategies, all investors need to position their financial capital to provide them with the money they need to live comfortably — both today and in the future. Without a well-developed and carefully maintained investment plan, investors risk not achieving their goals and failing to live the lives they want most.

For those reasons, chapters five through nine of this book are devoted to the investment planning process. Over the course of the next five chapters, you will learn (or be reminded of) the key principles used by highly successful investors to guide their decisions. For example:

1. **Beating the market is virtually impossible.** Most active money management strategies — such as stock picking and timing the markets — have consistently failed to add value or give investors an edge over the long term. This has held true in both bull and bear markets throughout history. In fact, financial markets operate in ways that make it extraordinarily tough for investors to beat them consistently.

2. **Owning a broadly-diversified portfolio of stocks is a prudent approach to investing.** The power of capitalism and free markets mean that it is not unreasonable for investors to expect stock prices to gradually rise over time.

3. **Risk and Return are Related.** Academic evidence suggests that there are at least three types of risk worth taking. The first is market risk: Stocks have outperformed bonds over time. The second is size risk: Shares of small companies have outperformed large-company stocks over time. The third is value risk: Value stocks (those with high book-to-market ratios) have generally outperformed growth stocks (those with low book-to-market ratios) over time. By taking these risks, investors may potentially generate stronger returns in their portfolios.

4. **Structured diversification can reduce volatility and enhance wealth.** It's impossible to know with certainty when an asset class will outperform all others and when it will underperform. Structured diversification — owning a mix of assets that have dissimilar price movements and overweighting equities and small and value company stocks — helps ensure that your portfolio is not over-exposed to any single asset class that is performing poorly at a given moment. The result: Your portfolio should experience more consistent returns from year to year instead of more dramatic swings in value — which, in turn, could enable your investments to build greater wealth for you over the long run.

5. **Building an ideal portfolio depends on each investor's risk capacity, risk tolerance and investment preferences.** Building a portfolio that is right for you will depend on your goals, income needs and time horizon. You'll also need to consider factors such as your feelings about market volatility, your reaction to potential declines in the value of your portfolio, and the types of investments and asset classes that you prefer to own in pursuit of your objectives.

6. **A disciplined long-term perspective is the key to staying on track and realizing your key financial goals.** Once your portfolio is created, let it do its job. That means staying invested instead of trying to time market movements, avoiding unnecessary trading and shutting down the many emotional and behavioral reactions to economic and market developments that can lead to costly mistakes.

It also requires a system of regular portfolio rebalancing to ensure that your portfolio's desired risk/return characteristics remain in place. Investors can maintain their disciplined approach by taking advantage of resources such as investment policy statements to help stay on track.

Some of the information contained in the following chapters will no doubt be familiar — while some may surprise you. By the end, we believe you will understand what it takes to build and maintain an investment plan that maximizes your chances of achieving your goals.

CHAPTER 5

Markets Work

Few things are more exciting to investors than the prospect of beating the market. If you can pick the right stocks and navigate your way successfully in and out of various market sectors at the right times, or find money managers to do the job for you, you'll generate outsized returns that will get you to your goals faster and help you achieve the lifestyle you desire. Not to mention that you'll get to brag to your friends and associates about the fortune you're making.

It's a wonderful and highly-appealing idea. Unfortunately, it suffers from a fatal flaw: History suggests that it's virtually impossible for even experienced money managers to beat the market consistently. We believe that by attempting to do so, you could put your financial dreams, goals and wealth at greater risk.

We realize that this probably isn't the first time you've been told that your chances of beating the market are extremely slim. We find that most investors understand and believe this on some level. But beating the market is such a tempting proposition that they often forget. And when the markets run into trouble — as they did in recent years — there's always a resurgence of the idea that "things have changed" or "it's different this time," which causes many investors to look for ways to try and outperform the market as a whole.

Very few sources of information that investors access — such as financial advisors, the media and even academics — take the time to explain how financial markets work. In this chapter, we'll show you not only that the markets are incredibly difficult to beat, but also why that's the case — regardless of whether we're in a raging bull market or a volatile bear market.

Our point is not simply to show that investors' attempts to beat the market are largely futile. We believe that you don't need to beat the market to enjoy success as an investor. In fact, we think that the alternative approach — capturing the overall rates of return offered by the market's major asset classes — may help put you in a stronger position to address the major challenges you face and achieve the meaningful goals you've set for yourself, as part of the wealth management consultative process.

The Case Against Active Management

Who wouldn't want to outperform the market? Certainly many investors and money managers devote a great deal of time and energy trying. But all the long-term historical data boil down to one inescapable conclusion: Trying to outperform the stock market's overall rate of return by actively trading stocks or engaging in market timing — has seldom succeeded over the long run.

Consider some of the most recent evidence from what has become a huge body of research over the years:

- **Active management fails over short periods.** A recent study by Standard & Poor's Index vs. Active Group (SPIVA) found that the S&P 500, the well-known unmanaged index of large U.S. stocks, outperformed 62 percent of actively managed large-capitalization mutual funds during the five years through 2010. Meanwhile, the S&P Small Cap 600, an unmanaged index of small U.S. stocks, performed better than 63 percent of actively managed small-cap stock mutual funds during that period. The results were even more dramatic among non-U.S. stocks. The S&P 700, an unmanaged index of international shares, beat 82 percent of actively managed international stock funds (See Exhibit 5.1).

Exhibit 5.1: Active Mutual Fund Manager 5-Year Performance from 2006 – 2010

Active Money Managers Have Difficulty Beating the Market

56%	62%	63%	82%
of intermediate fixed income managers underperformed the Barclays Intermediate Government/ Credit Bond Index	of large-cap managers underperformed the S&P 500 Index	of small-cap managers underperformed the S&P SmallCap 600 Index	of international managers underperformed the S&P700 Index

Source: Standard and Poor's Index Versus Active Group, March 2011 (For the period 1/05 – 12/09)

Indexes are not available for direct investment. Their performance does not reflect the expenses associated with the management of an actual portfolio. The fund returns used are net of fees, excluding loads. Returns are based upon equal-weighted fund counts. The data assumes reinvestment of income and does not account for taxes or transaction costs. The risks associated with stocks potentially include increased volatility (up and down movement in the value of your assets) and loss of principal. Bonds are subject to risks, including interest rate risk which can decrease the value of a bond as interest rates rise. Investing in foreign securities may involve certain additional risks, including exchange rate fluctuations, less liquidity, greater volatility, different financial and accounting standards and political instability. Past performance is not a guarantee of future results.

Additionally, the majority of actively managed funds in seven common equity categories underperformed their various benchmark indices during the five years through December 2010 (see Exhibit 5.2).

Exhibit 5.2: **Percentage of Active Public Equity Funds that Failed to Beat Their Indices**

(January 2006 – December 2010)

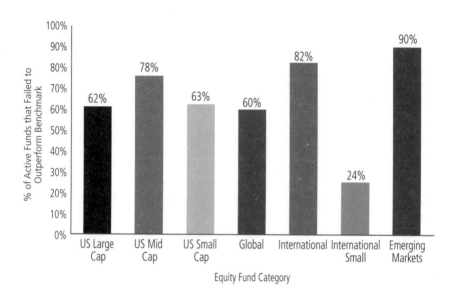

Source: Standard & Poor's Indices Versus Active Funds Scorecard, March 2011. Index used for comparison: US Large Cap — S&P 500 Index; US Mid Cap — S&P MidCap 400 Index; US Small Cap — S&P SmallCap 600 Index; Global Funds — S&P Global 1200 Index; International — S&P 700 Index; International Small — S&P Developed ex. US SmallCap Index; Emerging Markets — S&P IFCI Composite. Data for the SPIVA study is from the CRSP Survivor-Bias-Free US Mutual Fund Database.

Exhibit 5.3: **Percentage of Active Managers Who Outperform Due to Skill**

Universe of Active Mutual Fund Managers 1975-2006

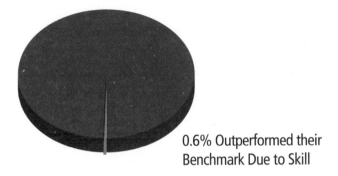

0.6% Outperformed their
Benchmark Due to Skill

- **Active management fails over long periods.** In a 2008 research study[12] — perhaps the most comprehensive ever performed — a team of professors used advanced statistical analysis to evaluate the performance of active mutual funds. They looked at fund performance over a 32-year period, from 1975-2006.

The study concluded that after expenses, only 0.6% (1 in 160) of active mutual funds actually outperformed the market through the money manager's skill (see Exhibit 5.3). The study concluded that this low number "can't eliminate the possibility that the few [funds] that did were merely false positives." In other words, they were just lucky.

Recent research, conducted by Eugene Fama of the University of Chicago and Kenneth French of Dartmouth, further supports these findings of luck versus skill.[13] In their research, they found that managers of actively managed funds, as a whole, possess only enough skill to cover their trading costs. Fama and French conducted 10,000

---

12 Barras, Laurent, Scaillet ,Wermers, and Russ, "False Discoveries in Mutual Fund Performance: Measuring Luck in Estimated Alphas" (May 2008).

13 Fama, Eugene F. and French, Kenneth R., Luck Versus Skill in the Cross Section of Mutual Fund Returns (December 14, 2009). Tuck School of Business Working Paper No. 2009-56 ; Chicago Booth School of Business Research Paper; Journal of Finance, Forthcoming. Available at SSRN: ssrn.com/abstract=1356021

simulations of the effect of luck on fund returns and found that, "The challenge is to distinguish skill from luck. Given the multitude of funds, many have extreme returns by chance."

Despite the existence of these lucky few outliers, Fama and French concluded that very few fund managers have superior enough skills to beat their indices, once costs were taken into consideration.

The research is further evidence that the majority of strong performing managers are simply lucky rather than skillful traders and that top-performing managers are unlikely to noticeably outperform large index funds in the future.

The inability of active money managers to beat their respective market indices isn't limited to stocks. As seen in Exhibit 5.4, the vast majority of active fixed-income managers — close to 100% in some instances — have failed to outperform their benchmarks.

Exhibit 5.4: **Percentage of Active Fixed Income Funds that Failed to Beat Their Indices**
January 2006 – December 2010

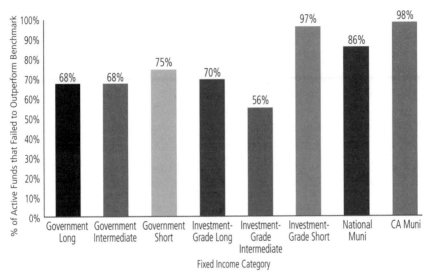

Source: Standard & Poor's Indices Versus Active Funds Scorecard, March 2011. Index used for comparison: Government Long — Barclays Capital US Long Government Index; Government Intermediate — Barclays Capital US Intermediate Government Index; Government Short — Barclays Capital US 1-3 Year Government Index; Investment Grade Long — Barclays Capital US Long Government/Credit; Investment Grade Intermediate — Barclays Capital US Intermediate Government/ Credit; Investment Grade Short — Barclays Capital US 1-3 Year Government/Credit; National Muni — S&P National Municipal Bond Index; CA Muni — S&P California Municipal Bond Index. Data for the SPIVA study is from the CRSP Survivor-Bias-Free US Mutual Fund Database. Barclays Capital data, formerly Lehman Brothers, provided by Barclays Bank PLC.

The evidence leads to three conclusions: 1) Historically, it has been extremely difficult for most active management strategies to outperform the market over short periods such as five years, 2) Most active managers have also failed to outperform the market over long periods and 3) A successful investment experience is not dependent on outperforming the market.

These points are especially important to keep in mind. After all, many of your most important goals in life are a decade or more away — such as ensuring that you have enough money to see you through a retirement that could last twenty or thirty years or even longer.

What About Bear Markets?

Some investors believe that while active managers will always have a tough time beating the market when times are good, active managers' market-beating abilities will be revealed during bear markets when lots of negative trends are hurting the market. Stock pickers and market timers, the argument goes, can use their intelligence and insight to sidestep the worst stocks with the poorest prospects or avoid entire asset classes and sectors that stand to get pummeled during a downturn.

Unfortunately, for these active managers, the research shows otherwise. For evidence, we only have to look as far back as 2008 — the year of the Great Recession, that saw U.S. stocks (as represented by the S&P 500 Index) plummet 37 percent in the wake of the worst global financial crisis since the 1930s. That year, actively managed funds as a group underperformed the S&P 500 by an average of 1.6 percent (see Exhibit 5.5). SPIVA also found similar results in 2003 when it reviewed the performance of actively managed funds during the 2000 to 2002 bear market.

Exhibit 5.5: Active Manager Performance During the 2008 Bear Market

Average U.S.
Equity Fund
Manager
Underperformed
S&P 500 by
1.67%

Source: Standard and Poor's Investment Service, May 2009. Indexes are not available for direct investment. Their performance does not reflect the expenses associated with the management of an actual portfolio.. The data assumes reinvestment of income and does not account for taxes or transaction costs. Past performance is not a guarantee of future results.

Why Has Active Management Failed So Often?

The case against active management is compelling. Yet many investors have a difficult time accepting the facts. It's extremely tempting to think that if we make smart investment decisions we can outperform the market — or find a hard-working, brilliant money manager or advisor who can do the job for us. After all, just because many active managers have struggled to beat the market in the past doesn't mean that someone won't be able to do so in the future, right? If you can find that manager and give him or her all your money today, you'll be rich in no time.

We understand how powerful and motivating that idea can be when making investment decisions. To be honest, there's nothing we'd like better than to find a manager who could beat the market year in and year out for decades and make us fabulously wealthy, too.

The problem with this thinking is that the financial markets operate in ways that make beating them extraordinarily difficult, even for the world's smartest managers. Specifically, there are five challenges that active managers face in trying to outperform the overall market:

Challenge 1: Success Requires Predictive Ability

Wall Street and the popular financial press want you to believe that in order to make money in the market, you need to invest based on what's about to happen. That's the message sent out every day by market strategists, brokers, analysts, mutual fund managers and the media — *predict the future accurately, and you'll score big.*

In truth, there is no crystal ball when it comes to investing your money. No one can accurately forecast market movements on a consistent basis over the long term. Why? Because we're talking about the future, and the future is by its very nature and definition *unknowable*. We simply cannot know *with certainty* the future direction of the economy, stock prices or the myriad events and developments that will occur that will have an impact on the markets.

Ah, but what about the countless PhDs and other experts on Wall Street who devote their time to sizing up economic and market developments and using their insights to make predictions? Surely they must have an ability to gauge the future that the rest of us lack?

For the answer, consider the following Wall Street predictions for where the S&P 500 would stand on December 31, 2008:

Morgan Stanley	1520
Merrill Lynch	1525
A.G. Edwards	1575
Wachovia Securities	1590
JP Morgan Chase	1590
Bank of America Securities	1625
Goldman Sachs	1675
Citigroup	1675
Strategas Research Partners	1680

For the record, the S&P 500 ended 2008 at 903.[14] In other words, none of these highly experienced firms, with access to a wealth of resources and information was able to predict even the down direction of the market that year.

Or take something as seemingly simple as predicting how the broad economy is going to do. As the *New York Times* noted in a May 5, 2009 article, "Amazingly enough, Wall Street's consensus forecast has failed to predict a single recession in the last 30 years."[15]

The media's track record is equally abysmal. One of the most famous examples is *Business Week's* August 13, 1979 cover story, "The Death of Equities." The article inside reached the conclusion that "The death of equities looks like an almost permanent condition — reversible someday, but not soon."

(For the record, the next decade was one of the strongest performing periods for the stock market in history, with the S&P 500 up 17.5 percent annually.)

For a more recent example, consider this advice from a February, 2009 *Forbes* article:

"It's way too early to get back into U.S. stocks…Expect meltdowns in securities backed by credit card debt, home equity, student and auto loans as well as commercial real estate…Avoid emerging markets, especially China."[16]

(For the record, U.S. stocks as measured by the S&P 500 soared 26.5 percent in 2009, emerging markets as a group shot up 79 percent and the Chinese market rose 62.6 percent.)

We could literally fill this book with hundreds of examples of various financial experts and gurus getting it wrong year after year after year. The upshot: Even the brightest analysts, the most famous, highly regarded money managers in the world or the most plugged-in and well-respected financial publications can seldom tell you what's going to happen next, let alone give you reliable advice on how to position your portfolio to take advantage. That doesn't mean that a fund manager, a talking head on CNBC or the guy who walks his dog down your street every morning won't sometimes get it right. They will. The credit, however, as we've seen, usually goes to luck — not skill. And your financial future is too important to leave to chance.

---

14 Source: USA Today. 2008 predictions for the S&P 500. January 2, 2008.

15 www.nytimes.com/2009/05/06/business/economy/06leonhardt.html

16 www.forbes.com/forbes/2009/0216/106.html

Challenge 2: The Market Doesn't Give Investors Many Opportunities To Beat It

Every day, there are millions of participants in the stock market. The majority are professional money managers, analysts, strategists and traders with advanced degrees who spend the bulk of their day doing one thing: trying to determine the accurate price of the stocks they're looking to buy and sell. These investors make their judgments by learning all they can about each company: Examining corporate documents and financial statements, reading analysts' reports and articles about the firms, listening to conference calls with management, and watching the news for developments about the companies, their suppliers and their competitors as well as the overall economy.

In other words, all these market participants use all the available information that exists to come up with their opinion of the right price. Investors looking to sell believe the price should be lower than the current price, while potential buyers believe the current price is too low. As a result, the market participants are constantly negotiating a "fair" price at which they're willing to strike a deal. It's a bit like selling your home and negotiating back and forth with a potential buyer to reach an acceptable price. When both parties agree — a willing seller finds a willing buyer — the transaction closes. Multiply that by millions of transactions every day, and you've got the stock market.

The fact that so many market participants are constantly processing huge amounts of new information to arrive at a fair price means that most stocks are priced efficiently — that is, the price of any stock at any given moment accurately reflects all the known information about it. Whenever any new information comes out, it gets seen and processed by millions of investors at essentially the same time. That causes the price of the stock to almost instantly rise or fall to a new agreed upon "fair" value that once again reflects all the current knowledge about that stock.

As an investor, this means you should generally accept that the price of any stock at a given moment is the price it should be. Why? Because it reflects the collective knowledge of all the investors in the market at that point in time. Naturally, then, the value of the stock market as a whole is accurate at any moment. After all, if those millions of buyers and sellers didn't think prices were fair, no one would ever make a trade. But the fact that more than 8,000 listed stocks change hands every day in the U.S. proves a crucial point: Capital markets are efficient. They allow buyers and sellers to make trades at prices that the participants deem to be fair.

The result of this market efficiency is that the market doesn't easily present any single investor or group of investors with a huge opportunity for outsized profits. Think about it this way: Let's say you are a professional investor with a huge brain and an unflagging work ethic who is trying to beat the market. To do that, you need to uncover opportunities that the other investors don't see. The challenge is, you're surrounded on all sides — on all continents, really — by a million other extremely smart, incredibly hard-working investors who are also looking to uncover opportunities that go unnoticed. Meanwhile, thanks to technology, all of you are receiving and viewing the same new financial information about companies and the economy at once. Given all that, you would eventually have to ask a key question: What are the chances that you'll see a mistake — a mispricing, in other words — that some or all of your 999,999 colleagues, peers and competitors won't?

Challenge 3: Profiting From Occasional Mispricings Is Tough

That said, just because markets are efficient doesn't mean that market participants are perfectly rational and always make optimal decisions. It's possible that inefficiencies — mispricings — could appear from time to time, as investors' emotions get the best of them and they make judgments about the market based on greed or fear. This concept was most recently evidenced in 2008 and early 2009. Markets plunged, in part because most of the new information that was coming out during that time was extremely negative, but also because much of that new information was unclear and created a huge amount of uncertainty. Investors, left with information that they didn't always know how to process, panicked and drove the market deep into bear territory.

In that environment, an investor might have gone against the herd by aggressively buying stocks when they were severely beaten down — and generated huge gains, when, starting in March 2009 the stock market began to soar. With the benefit of hindsight, you might even claim that any idiot could have seen how mispriced the market was and that stocks were a screaming bargain.

But here's an interesting fact. Although any number of investors could have done exactly those things, they didn't. In fact, they did the exact opposite — they sold stocks and bought bonds. What we witnessed was the same fear that prompted investors to sell stocks when times were bleak also stopped them from buying stocks when they were "cheap" and offered the potential for outsized gains. Therefore, the vast majority of investors missed the opportunity to fully participate in stock market's surprising 2009 surge. The result was — you guessed it — that they missed an amazing opportunity to take part in a tremendous market rally and potentially make a lot of money.

It's not just emotions that make it difficult to take advantage of the occasional mispricing. Once again, think of yourself as that professional investor trying to uncover hidden opportunities. As noted before, in order to generate a market-beating return, you would first need to identify a mistake that everyone else fails to see. But that's just step one. Next, that mistake would have to stay around long enough for you to do something about it — another highly unlikely scenario. But let's say that occurs. You "get it right" by buying the stock that you and you alone have identified as mistakenly priced too low by the rest of the world. You're still not done. You have to sell that stock at just the right time to a buyer just before it dips in value. In other words, to win you have to "get it right" not once, but twice.

Keep in mind that this is just one example. If you or your money manager want to beat the market consistently, you need to make a habit of finding mispricings that last long enough to trade on them and then "get it right twice." Having one great idea isn't going to allow you to beat the market and make you wealthy. You may very well get lucky once or even a few times. But how likely is it that you'll get lucky month after month, year after year for decades? Of course, you already know the answer from Exhibit 5.3 above: Less than one percent of active mutual fund managers had the skill to outperform the broader market over the 32-year period from 1975 through 2006. As an investor with a lengthy time horizon, you need to honestly assess whether you think you, or your investment managers, fall into that tiny group. Odds are you and your managers won't.

Bottom line: While there may very well be occasional mispricings in the financial markets, there's very little you or anyone can do to actually profit from those inefficiencies consistently enough to have a positive impact on your wealth. The smart move is therefore to act as if those mispricings don't exist.

Challenge 4: The Market's Returns Are Driven By A Select Group Of Stocks That Is Always Changing

You know that stocks overall have delivered positive returns over the long run. What you might not realize is that a relatively small group of stocks has been responsible for that positive return.

For example, looking at the University of Chicago's CRSP total market equity database as representative of the U.S. market for the period 1926-2009, we find that only the top-performing 25% of stocks were responsible for the market gains during this timeframe. The remaining 75% of the stocks in the total market database collectively generated a loss of -0.6%. (see Exhibit 5.6).

Exhibit 5.6: The Impact on Returns of Missing the Top-Performing Stocks (1926-2009)

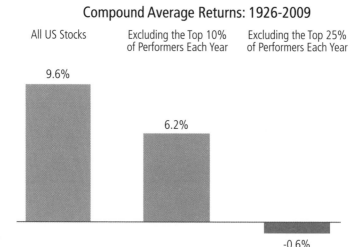

Compound Average Returns: 1926-2009

Source: Dimensional Fund Advisors. Past performance is not indicative of future results. Indexes are unmanaged baskets of securities in which investors cannot directly invest. The data assume reinvestment of all dividend and capital gain distributions; they do not include the effect of any taxes, transaction costs or fees charged by an investment advisor or other service provider to an individual account. The risks associated with stocks potentially include increased volatility (up and down movement in the value of your assets) and loss of principal. Small company stocks may be subject to a higher degree of market risk than the securities of more established companies because they tend to be more volatile and less liquid.

The common response from some investors to this statistic is: If a small percentage of stocks could possibly account for the market's long-term returns, why not avoid all the headaches and just invest in these top performing stocks? You know the answer, of course. It's the one written on every prospectus you've ever received: "Past performance is not indicative of future results" — and we know that no one can predict the future with perfect accuracy. A portfolio of even the most carefully screened stocks could easily wind up with none of the best-performing stocks in the market — and thus could possibly produce flat or negative returns over time. As the performance of active managers in Exhibits 5.2 and 5.4 above showed, very few of them are accomplished stock pickers. Missing out on even a handful of the top-performing stocks can leave you well short of market returns.

Clearly there is great difficulty and danger inherent in selecting individual stocks. If you had tried to pick winners and avoid losers during the timeframe cited above, you would have put yourself at great risk of not owning the small group of stocks that drove most of the market's return. In essence, you would have been trying to seek out a few needles in an enormous haystack. If you got it right, you did great. If you got it wrong, you did very, very poorly. Either way, the results would have been the same: You would have failed to beat the market.

Conversely, you could have sought out a smart fund manager who you hoped could pick the stocks that would fall into that top 25 percent category over the long term — or better yet, pick just the best performers from among that select group of winners. But once again, the data tells us that almost no one has been capable of beating the market consistently over long periods of time. By trying to find the tiny handful of managers who might be capable of doing so from among the thousands of professional managers in the business, you'd once again be seeking a small number of needles in a huge haystack.

Challenge 5: Trying To Beat The Market Is Expensive

A final challenge to active management is that returns for active mutual funds may be reduced by higher expenses, since active funds often charge substantial fees and incur heavy trading and tax costs in the efforts to actively move in and out of markets, select specific stocks and "be right twice." The truth is, all those smart and hard-working professionals — the ones who can't seem to beat the market — don't come cheap. In one study, Kenneth R. French, a professor of finance at Dartmouth College's Tuck School of Business, added up the fees and expenses of U.S. equity mutual funds, investment management costs paid by institutions, fees paid to hedge funds, and the transaction costs paid by all traders in 2006. Then he deducted what U.S. equity investors would have paid if instead, they had simply bought and held an index fund benchmarked against the overall stock market. The difference between these amounts — the amount that investors pay trying (and failing) to beat the market — was a whopping $102 billion.[17]

A better approach: Accept the market rate of return — it has plenty to offer.

Remember, our goal is to help give you a framework you can utilize to make the smartest possible decisions about your money so you can achieve all that is important to you. One of the smartest decisions you can make is to avoid doing things that history has shown don't work. And the evidence is clear: Trying to beat the market through active management techniques like stock picking and market timing is a real challenge.

The good news is that you don't have to beat the market in order to be a successful investor. Instead, you can take a much smarter, more effective and simpler approach: Own the entire market and stay invested through thick and thin. We saw how missing just a few stocks can diminish your returns. That means the only way you can be assured of owning all of tomorrow's top-performing stocks is to own the entire market all the time.

If you do that, you stand a much better chance to capture the rate of return that the market has historically generated over time. The less you do to put that positive historical return at risk, the better your chances of coming out ahead in the end.

Here's why: The common goal of all publicly-traded companies is to earn money and maximize the value they provide to their shareholders — the people who own stock in their companies. Some of these companies fail to generate earnings and eventually go out of business. Other companies succeed wildly. On balance, more companies have created wealth than destroyed it. We know this because if more companies destroyed wealth than created it, our economy wouldn't grow. Capital markets would have essentially "gone out of business" long ago. But in fact, the exact opposite has occurred.

A portfolio of stocks is more than the actual shares themselves — it's a sign of confidence that, for example, Starbucks will continue to serve a cup of coffee for $2. If you invest your money in shares of publicly-traded companies, you literally own a stake in the wealth that they may create. And as companies create more and more wealth, investors become increasingly willing to pay higher prices to own a piece of that wealth.

This proposition — that you can succeed by joining your fortunes to the future of U.S. and global industry — is hugely powerful. We believe this means that it is prudent and rational to expect stock prices to gradually keep rising over time. We think the market should produce a long-term positive rate of return because wealth will continue to be created by companies, and stock prices reflect that continual creation of wealth. It means that investing in stocks is not akin to gambling with your money in the hope of making a profit. It's investing in the belief that profits will still be made, that innovation will still occur and that companies will continue to find ways to make money going forward.

---

17   Kenneth R. French, "The Cost of Active Investing," March 2008.

That's not to say there won't be blips, speed bumps and the occasional enormous potholes along the way — there most certainly will be. But if you believe in the power of innovation and invest accordingly, you have the opportunity to participate in any rewards and growth that result.

The rates of return you may receive as an investor in the entire market will be different for each type of company, depending on the level of risk that is involved in generating its wealth. For example, small firms that are just starting out are generally riskier for investors than large firms that dominate their industries. That's one reason why shares of small publicly traded companies have outperformed shares of the largest firms over time.

To illustrate, Exhibit 5.7 shows the annualized return of 13 different types of publicly traded companies from 1926 – 2010, as categorized by the Center for Research in Security Prices. Decile indices one, two, three, four and five represent the largest companies that trade in the U.S. market (with decile one representing the very largest firms). Decile indices six, seven, eight, nine and ten represent small companies (with decile ten representing the smallest of the small). The Deciles 1-10 Index represents the entire market, the Deciles 1-5 Index represents large-cap stocks as a group, and the Deciles 6-10 Index represented small-cap stocks as a group.

Exhibit 5.7: **The Long-Term Annualized Returns of 13 Asset Classes**

Annualized Returns 1926 - 2010

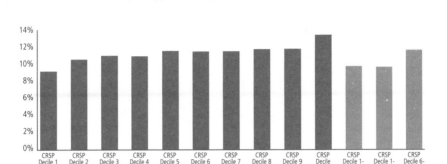

Source: Center for Research in Security Prices, 2011. Past performance is no guarantee of future results.

Our message is that you shouldn't spend your time and energy picking the right stocks or hunting for the winning manager to achieve your goals. The alternative — investing in assets classes — offers you a simple, straight forward and broadly-diversified approach and frees you from having to worry about the ups and downs of individual stocks.

In the end, we can't force you to invest one way or the other. The choice is yours. But given the tremendous challenges that an active management approach faces, you at least have to ask yourself if it's the most sensible approach to take. If your managers can accomplish the task, you'll be in great shape. If they can't — and there's no doubt that the chances of this are slim — then you expose yourself and your family to the risk of earning below-market returns.

Is it worth the risk? We believe it isn't.

CHAPTER 6

Risk & Return Are Related

So far we've seen that taking certain types of risks, such as trying to pick winning stocks — and avoiding the losers — and attempting to time markets, have historically failed to generate market-beating returns over the long run. In fact, they may have left many investors with less money than they had originally.

The good news is that there are other types of risk that you may want to consider taking. Markets can be chaotic, but over time they have shown a strong relationship between risk and reward. This means that the compensation for taking on increased levels of risk is the potential to earn greater returns. In fact, when it comes to investing, the return your portfolio earns will be substantially driven by the overall amount of risk you take. But all risks aren't created equal.

According to noted academic research, there are three "factors" or sources of potentially higher returns with higher corresponding risks:[18]

1. Stocks (market risk)

2. Small Companies (size risk)

3. Value Companies (value risk)

---

18 Cross Section of Expected Stock Returns", Eugene F. Fama and Kenneth R. French, Journal of Finance 47 (1992).

These risks were identified and tested by two professors, Eugene Fama and Ken French, in the early 1990s. Their research resulted in what is known as the Fama-French Three-Factor Model, which has become the basis for portfolio construction for many top investors (See Exhibit 6.1). One of the most important jobs for an advisor or investor is to understand the risk factors contained in this model in order to decide how to incorporate them into your portfolio.

Exhibit 6.1: **Three-Factor Model**

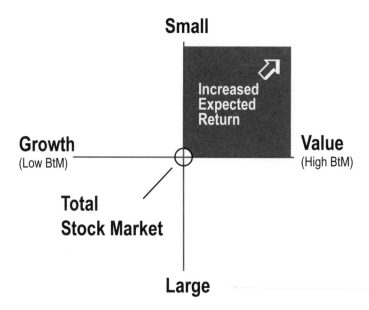

Risk 1: Market Risk

Market risk is the risk of investing in the equity market versus investing in a "riskless asset," such as a 30-day Treasury Bill. Stock investors demand a higher rate of return than investors who buy government bonds in order to compensate them for the increased risk of holding equities. While past performance is no guarantee of future results, stocks as a whole have outperformed bonds and Treasury bills by a large margin over the last eight decades.[19] As seen in Exhibit 6.2, $1 invested in stocks in 1927 would have grown to $2,577 by the end of 2010 — while that same investment in T-bills would have grown to a mere $20.

Exhibit 6.2: Stocks Outperform Bonds Over Time 1927 - 2010

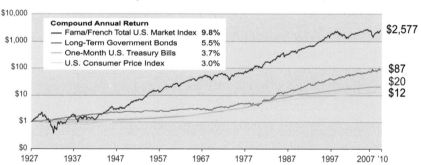

Source: Morningstar's 2010 Stocks, Bonds, Bills, And Inflation Yearbook (2011); Fama/French Total U.S. Market Index provided by Fama/French from Center for Research in Security Prices (CRSP) data. Includes all NYSE securities (plus Amex equivalents since July 1962 and NASDAQ equivalents since 1973), including utilities. Risks associated with investing in stocks potentially include increased volatility (up and down movement in the value of your assets) and loss of principal. Indexes are unmanaged baskets of securities that investors cannot directly invest in. Past performance is no guarantee of future results. Hypothetical value of $1 invested at the beginning of 1927 and kept invested through December 31, 2010. Assumes reinvestment of income and no transaction costs or taxes. This is for illustrative purposes only and not indicative of any investment. An investment cannot be made directly in an index.

---

19 Represented by the Fama/French Total U.S. Market Index, which consists of all the securities listed on the New York Stock Exchange plus American Stock Exchange equivalents since July 1962 and NASDAQ equivalents since 1973.

Also called "systematic risk," market risk cannot be minimized or eliminated through diversification — in other words, if you invest in stocks, you must be willing to accept market risk. By contrast, unsystematic risk — the risk that's inherent in investing in a single company or even a group of companies in a single industry — can be mitigated by diversification. In a market like 2008, the risk of concentrating on a single stock or sector was a potential invitation to catastrophe.

The relationship between risk and return makes sense. Investors can buy a short-term Treasury bill, which is essentially a loan to the U.S. government, and take minimal risk. Or they can invest in the broad stock market — in other words, own a piece of many companies and their current and future profits. As a partial owner of public companies, you accept more risk than if you are simply a lender to the government — and you should expect a greater return because of your willingness to accept that additional risk.

This relationship also extends to bonds issued by corporations. If a company declares bankruptcy, its bondholders may be able to recover some or all of their original investment. Stockholders have less likelihood of recovering their investment, as their claims are subordinate to those of bondholders. Because of additional risk, stockholders have tended to demand a higher return than bondholders.

Investing in the stock market carries risk that doesn't always reward you year in and year out. There have been several long periods when bonds outperformed stocks — most recently, for example, the 10-year period through 2010 saw the Fama/French Total U.S. Market Index return 2.6 percent annually while the BofA Merrill Lynch 1-3 Year Treasury/Agency Index gained 4.0 percent.

The good news, however, is that historically, investors have been compensated for their willingness to take on market risk over the long term.

Risk 2: Size Risk

One common way investors categorize stocks is by size. Large-company stocks are shares of firms with large market capitalizations (defined as the stock's price per share multiplied by the number of shares outstanding), while small-company stocks have small market capitalizations. A large company might be an international firm with tens of thousands of employees. A small firm could have just a few hundred or even several dozen employees.

When dividing the entire stock market by size, we see that small-company stocks have tended to reward investors with significantly higher returns over time than large-company shares. In Exhibit 6.3, CRSP Decile 1 stocks are the largest U.S. stocks while CRSP Decile 10 contains the smallest U.S. stocks. Notice the clear relationship between risk and reward — the smaller the stocks, the higher the returns. Indeed, the very smallest stocks (Decile 10) have significantly outperformed all other stocks from 1926 - 2010.

Exhibit 6.3: **Small-Caps Outperform Large-Caps Over Time**

Return-Standard Deviation
Monthly: January 1926 - December 2010; Default Currency: USD

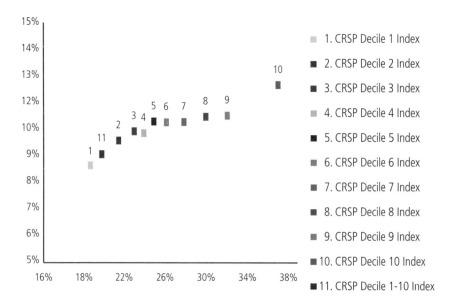

The Center for Research in Security Prices (CRSP) ranks all NYSE companies by market capitalization and divides them into 10 equally-populated portfolios. AMEX and NASDAQ National Market stocks are then placed into deciles according to their respective capitalizations, determined by the NYSE breakpoints. CRSP Portfolios 6-10 represent small caps. Standard deviation is a statistical measurement of how far the return of a security (or index) moves above or below its average value. The greater the standard deviation, the riskier an investment is considered to be.

Why is this the case?

Simple: Small-company stocks are riskier than large company stocks. Smaller firms typically are younger and less financially stable than their larger, older peers. Smaller firms also tend to be located in smaller geographic areas and are less able to withstand economic downturns. They also tend to have less stable or consistent earnings from year to year than the largest, most established firms. For example, compare Starbucks with a hypothetical smaller, upstart competitor, who we'll call for the sake of this example: New Brews.

Smaller firms (like New Brews) have the potential to grow into giants (like Starbucks). But they also are more likely to go out of business if they experience problems; their lesser size and capital base mean they have a smaller financial cushion to help them weather a downturn in business conditions. Because of these risks, investors demand a higher return when they buy shares of small companies. The risk that Starbucks will implode is relatively low. After all, they're on practically every street corner in America. As a result, investors in Starbucks are willing to accept a relatively low return on their investment. However, the risk that New Brews will implode is significantly higher. Investors will only buy shares in New Brews if they can reasonably expect to earn a higher return to compensate them for incurring additional risk. In short, if New Brews didn't offer a higher potential return, do you think any investors would choose them over Starbucks?

But just like in the example in Market Risk above, small-company stocks do not always outperform large-company stocks. In fact, many years can go by during which this size premium reverses and shares of larger firms beat shares of smaller companies — sometimes by very significant margins. However, as you can see from Exhibit 6.4, small-company stocks have historically outperformed their larger peers over time. In fact, small stocks beat large stocks 88% of the time over rolling 20-year periods from June, 1926 through 2010, and 97% of the time over rolling 25-year periods.

Exhibit 6.4: **US Small vs. US Large**
July 1926 - December 2010

In 25-Year Periods	Small beat large 97% of the time
In 20-Year Periods	Small beat large 88% of the time
In 15-Year Periods	Small beat large 82% of the time
In 10-Year Periods	Small beat large 75% of the time
In 5-Year Periods	Small beat large 59% of the time

Periods based on rolling annualized returns. 715 total 25-year periods. 775 total 20-year periods. 835 total 15-year periods. 895 total 10-year periods. 955 total 5-year periods. Indices are not available for direct investment. Their performance does not reflect the expenses associated with the management of an actual portfolio. Past performance is not a guarantee of future results. Indices used: Fama/French US Small Cap Index, Fama/French US Large Cap Index. The risks associated with investing in stocks and overweighting small company stocks potentially include increased volatility (up and down movement in the value of your assets) and loss of principal. Small-cap stocks may be less liquid than large-cap stocks.

Risk 3: Value Risk

A third type of risk identified by Fama and French's research pertains to growth stocks versus value stocks. Similar to how investors divide stocks into small and large, they also divide stocks by whether they fall into the "growth" category or the "value" category.

Value stocks are usually associated with corporations that have experienced slower earnings growth or sales, or have recently experienced business difficulties, causing their stock prices to fall. These value companies are often regarded as turnaround opportunities, where a change in management, strategy or other factors could improve the company's prospects and its earnings.

Historically, the earning streams of value stocks have been much more uncertain than growth stocks. This means the market has to assign them lower prices in order to attract investors.

Though they are riskier than growth companies, emphasizing value companies in a portfolio may lead to both increased diversification and the expectation of potentially higher returns.

In Exhibit 6.5, you can see how Value has fared versus Growth over various time periods.

Exhibit 6.5: **Value Outperforms Growth**
July 1926 - December 2010

In 25-Year Periods	Value beat growth 100% of the time
In 20-Year Periods	Value beat growth 100% of the time
In 15-Year Periods	Value beat growth 95% of the time
In 10-Year Periods	Value beat growth 91% of the time
In 5-Year Periods	Value beat growth 82% of the time

Periods based on rolling annualized returns. 715 total 25-year periods. 775 total 20-year periods. 835 total 15-year periods. 895 total 10-year periods. 955 total 5-year periods. Indices are not available for direct investment. Their performance does not reflect the expenses associated with the management of an actual portfolio. Past performance is not a guarantee of future results. Indices used on this chart: Fama/French US Large Value Index (ex utilities), Fama/French US Large Growth Index (ex utilities. The risks associated with investing in stocks and overweighting value stocks potentially include increased volatility (up and down movement in the value of your assets) and loss of principal.

Here again risk drives reward. In this case, consider the characteristics of value stocks: They are out of favor with investors, who see such firms as risky — especially when compared to growth companies, which are usually characterized by their high prices, strong earnings growth and high returns on equity.

In order to allocate investment capital to value stocks, investors demand greater compensation than they do from the more stable growth companies. If these value stocks didn't offer higher expected returns, no one would bother investing in them.

As an example, consider two well-known retailers: Sears and Wal-Mart. In recent years Sears has encountered numerous hurdles that caused its sales to significantly lag its competitors. In fact, Sears was actually bought by Kmart — the discount retailer that was in such bad financial shape in 2002 that it declared bankruptcy. By contrast, Wal-Mart experienced strong growth in sales and profits during the past decade and by many metrics would have to be considered superior to Sears (and Kmart).

And yet, as seen in Exhibit 6.6, Sears stock has delivered much higher returns than Wal-Mart stock during the past seven years or so. While Sears stock was up nearly 400% during that time, Wal-Mart stock was essentially flat. How can that possibly be the case? It's because Sears was a riskier investment than "sure-thing" Wal-Mart. Notice how volatile Sears' stock returns are compared to Wal-Mart's; that extra risk compensated investors with a much higher return.

Exhibit 6.6: Sears Stock Versus Wal-Mart Stock
May 2, 2003 - December 31, 2010

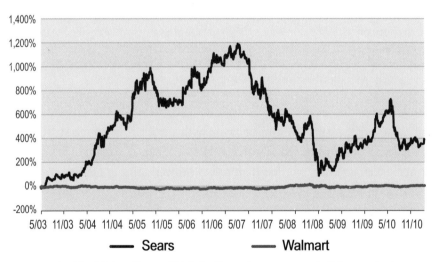

Source: Loring Ward; Yahoo Finance. This is for illustrative purposes only. This type of value vs. growth phenomena is not always the case. Value companies will not always outperform growth companies, and there have been historical periods when growth has significantly outpaced value.

Still, this idea that value stocks are riskier than growth stocks is hard for some investors to grasp. Many investors assume the opposite — that because innovative growth companies take bigger chances than distressed value companies they're riskier and therefore more likely to reward investors.

On first blush, this sounds reasonable. But remember that value stocks are stocks with low relative prices. Why? Because investors have pushed down value stocks' prices to compensate for all that risk. Value stocks have much greater earnings uncertainty than growth stocks, for example. In the face of this type of uncertainty, investors often sell value stocks driving their prices lower. Then, as many of these distressed companies solve their financial problems and become healthier, investors start to pay attention, buy the shares and drive up the prices. So even though it might sound a little strange, the "bad" value companies perform better as an investment than the "good" growth companies over the long run, as we saw Exhibit 6.5.

The risks that compensate investors domestically also are in evidence internationally. As you can see from Exhibit 6.7, from 1975 – 2010 in the international markets, value stocks have outperformed growth stocks — and small-cap stocks have outperformed large-cap stocks — in a majority of all rolling return periods measured. The value premium has been strongly positive more often than the size premium.

EXHIBIT 6.7: **International Risk Dimensions**
January 1975 - December 2010

In 25-Year Periods	Value beat growth 100% of the time
In 20-Year Periods	Value beat growth 100% of the time
In 15-Year Periods	Value beat growth 100% of the time
In 10-Year Periods	Value beat growth 100% of the time
In 5-Year Periods	Value beat growth 98% of the time
In 25-Year Periods	Small beat large 100% of the time
In 20-Year Periods	Small beat large 97% of the time
In 15-Year Periods	Small beat large 82% of the time
In 10-Year Periods	Small beat large 78% of the time
In 5-Year Periods	Small beat large 78% of the time

Based on rolling annualized returns. Rolling multi-year periods overlap and are not independent. This statistical dependence must be considered when assessing the reliability of long-horizon return differences. International Value vs. International Growth data: 133 overlapping 25-year periods. 193 overlapping 20-year periods. 253 overlapping 15-year periods. 313 overlapping 10-year periods. 373 overlapping 5-year periods. International Small vs. International Large data: 193 overlapping 25-year periods. 253 overlapping 20-year periods. 313 overlapping 15-year periods. 373 overlapping 10-year periods. 433 overlapping 5-year periods. International Value and Growth data provided by Fama/French from Bloomberg and MSCI securities data. International Small data compiled by Dimensional from Bloomberg, StyleResearch, London Business School, and Nomura Securities data. International Large is MSCI World ex USA Index gross of foreign withholding taxes on dividends; copyright MSCI 2011, all rights reserved. The risks associated with investing in stocks and overweighting small company and value stocks potentially include increased volatility (up and down movement in the value of your assets) and loss of principal. Small-cap stocks may be less liquid than large-cap stocks. Foreign securities involve additional risks including foreign currency changes, taxes and different accounting and financial reporting methods. All investments involve risk, including loss of principal.

What The Market, Size And Value Premiums Mean For Investors

The data in this chapter, culled from decades of research, is intended to help investors understand the risks that may generate returns. Research on financial markets is ongoing, and our knowledge will continue to expand. But what we do know about risk and return provide a sound framework for building and maintaining your portfolio. Your job doesn't need to be — nor should it be — focused on picking the right stocks and avoiding the wrong ones.

Instead, we believe your investment strategy should center around three major decisions. First, decide how much overall market risk you want and are able to take. That decision will impact how much money is allocated to stocks versus bonds, T-bills and cash. Then within the equity portion of your portfolio, do you want stocks to be larger or smaller on average than the overall market, and do you want them to be more value or growth oriented?

If you want and are able to take on more risk in pursuit of higher expected returns, you can increase your exposure to small-cap stocks, value stocks or both. If you're more concerned about safety and stability, you can increase your exposure to fixed income.

In the next chapter, we'll discuss specific diversification strategies that will help you keep your wealth management plan on track regardless of what the markets are doing.

CHAPTER 7

Diversify with Structure

The third component of successful investing is diversifying your portfolio across multiple types of assets and investments. Diversifying with structure enables investors to potentially reduce the overall risk in their portfolios and increase their portfolios' long-term potential returns over time.

Diversification is a well-known term, of course. But far too many investors still don't fully understand what it really means or even why they should take the time to build and maintain well-diversified portfolios. Even if you think you know all there is to know about diversification, we urge you to read this chapter so you can determine if your efforts at diversification are truly on target or if you need to reevaluate your approach. We will also introduce the concept of "diversifying with structure," which differs significantly from conventional approaches to diversification.

The Case for Diversification

Investors sometimes question the need for diversification. Instead of allocating their wealth by investing in a wide range of assets, investment styles, and markets, they ask, "Why not just put all your money in investments that have a history of beating other assets and the overall market?"

The reason, as anyone who lost sleep during the market meltdown of the "Great Recession" can tell you, is that no single type of asset always performs well. It's true that stocks, as measured by the Fama/French Total U.S. Market Index, have beaten all other asset classes over time, gaining 9.8 percent annually from 1927 through 2010.[20] But that superior return was of little

---

20 Risks associated with investing in stocks potentially include increased volatility (up and down movement in the value of your assets) and loss of principal. Indexes are unmanaged baskets of securities that investors cannot directly invest in. Past performance is no guarantee of future results. An investment cannot be made directly in an index. Fama/French Total U.S. Market Index provided by Fama/French from Center for Research in Security Prices (CRSP) data. Includes all NYSE securities (plus Amex equivalents since July 1962 and NASDAQ equivalents since 1973), including utilities.

comfort during the 2008 bear market when the S&P 500 index plummeted nearly 40 percent. Even the size and value premiums didn't pay off in 2008.

But remember: Investing is all about the future — what's going to happen. In order for you to successfully shift your money from one investment to the next, you would have to know what stock, sector or asset class is going to outperform the others going forward. And the future is, by its very nature, unknowable — none of us can be completely certain what is going to occur in the next five minutes, five days or five years. There will always be unanticipated events that affect the world and, therefore, your investments.

For example, ask yourself if you've ever had an investment that didn't work out. Why didn't it perform as planned? Because you (or the person managing your money) didn't anticipate a development that affected your investment. Every active money manager wants to beat the market — yet, so few actually do. We believe that no one — not even the brightest minds on Wall Street — can accurately predict the future time and time again. If they could, they'd beat the market year after year after year. As you saw in Chapter Five, that just hasn't happened.

The upshot: It's nearly impossible to know when an asset class will outperform and when it will fall to the bottom of the pack. Indeed, the asset class that wins the performance race in one year rarely is capable of defending its crown the next — and a losing asset class one year often unexpectedly soars to the top of list the next year. As you can see from Exhibit 7.1, in 1999, for example, emerging markets shares soared almost 66% and were the top-performing stock category for the year. The worst category that year was REITs, which fell 5%. But in the very next year, emerging markets fell to the bottom of the pack, declining 30%. The top performing category of 2000 was REITs, up 26%.

Exhibit 7.1: Asset Class Index Performance 1996-2010

1996	1997	1998	1999	2000	2001	2002	2003	2004	2005	2006	2007	2008	2009	2010	Annualized Returns
REITs 35.27%	Small Value 36.94%	Large Growth 36.65%	Emerging Markets 65.82%	REITs 26.37%	Small Value 40.59%	5 Year Gov't 12.95%	Small Value 74.48%	REITs 31.58%	Emerging Markets 29.32%	REITs 35.06%	Emerging Markets 36.87%	5 Year Gov't 13.11%	Emerging Markets 84.74%	Small Value 34.59%	Small Value 12.10%
S&P 500 Index 22.96%	Large Value 33.75%	S&P 500 Index 28.58%	Small Growth 54.06%	5 Year Gov't 12.60%	REITs 13.93%	REITs 3.82%	Emerging Markets 70.66%	Emerging Markets 28.00%	EAFE 13.54%	Emerging Markets 31.84%	Large Growth 15.70%	Inflation (CPI) 0.09%	Small Value 70.19%	Small Growth 31.83%	REITs 10.54%
Small Value 22.36%	S&P 500 Index 33.36%	EAFE 20.00%	Large Growth 30.16%	Inflation (CPI) 3.38%	5 Year Gov't 7.61%	Inflation (CPI) 2.39%	Small Growth 54.72%	Small Value 27.33%	REITs 12.16%	EAFE 26.34%	EAFE 11.17%	S&P 500 Index -37.00%	Large Growth 38.09%	REITs 27.96%	Emerging Markets 10.15%
Large Growth 21.27%	Large Growth 31.67%	Large Value 11.95%	EAFE 26.96%	Small Value -3.08%	Inflation (CPI) 1.55%	Emerging Markets -9.68%	EAFE 38.59%	EAFE 20.25%	Large Value 9.70%	Large Value 21.87%	5 Year Gov't 10.05%	REITs -37.73%	Small Growth 38.09%	Large Value 20.17%	S&P 500 Index 6.77%
Large Value 19.97%	REITs 20.26%	5 Year Gov't 10.22%	S&P 500 Index 21.04%	Large Value -5.41%	Small Value -2.71%	Small Value -11.72%	REITs 37.13%	Large Value 17.74%	Small Growth 6.02%	Small Value 21.70%	Large Value 5.49%	Large Growth -39.12%	Large Value 37.51%	Large Growth 17.64%	5 Year Gov't 5.82%
Small Growth 13.22%	Small Growth 14.88%	Small Growth 4.08%	Large Value 6.99%	S&P 500 Index -9.10%	Emerging Markets -3.65%	EAFE -15.94%	Large Value 36.43%	Small Growth 11.16%	S&P 500 Index 4.91%	S&P 500 Index 15.80%	Small Growth 4.99%	EAFE -43.38%	Small Growth 31.78%	Emerging Markets 17.34%	Large Growth 5.80%
Emerging Markets 10.83%	5 Year Gov't 8.38%	Inflation (CPI) 1.60%	Small Value 4.37%	EAFE -14.17%	Small Growth -4.13%	Large Growth -21.93%	S&P 500 Index 28.69%	S&P 500 Index 10.88%	Small Value 4.46%	Small Growth 9.26%	Inflation (CPI) 4.09%	Small Growth -43.41%	REITs 27.99%	S&P 500 Index 15.06%	Small Growth 5.16%
EAFE 6.05%	EAFE 1.78%	Emerging Markets -3.32%	Inflation (CPI) 2.68%	Large Growth -14.33%	S&P 500 Index -11.89%	S&P 500 Index -22.10%	Large Growth 17.77%	Large Growth 5.27%	Inflation (CPI) 3.42%	Large Growth 5.97%	Large Growth -12.24%	S&P 500 Index -44.50%	Small Value 26.46%	EAFE 7.75%	EAFE 4.70%
Inflation (CPI) 3.33%	Inflation (CPI) 1.70%	Small Value -10.04%	5 Year Gov't -1.76%	Small Growth -24.50%	Large Value -21.05%	Large Value -30.28%	5 Year Gov't 2.40%	Inflation (CPI) 3.25%	Large Growth 3.39%	5 Year Gov't 3.15%	REITs -15.69%	Emerging Markets -52.67%	Inflation (CPI) 2.72%	5 Year Gov't 7.12%	Large Value 3.92%
5 Year Gov't 2.09%	Emerging Markets -24.26%	REITs -17.50%	REITs -4.62%	Emerging Markets -30.40%	EAFE -21.44%	Small Growth -34.63%	Inflation (CPI) 1.88%	5 Year Gov't 2.26%	5 Year Gov't 1.35%	Inflation (CPI) 2.55%	Small Value -18.38%	Large Value -53.14%	5 Year Gov't -2.40%	Inflation (CPI) 1.50%	Inflation (CPI) 2.40%

High ↑ / Low ↓

Data Sources: Center for Research in Security Prices (CRSP), BARRA Inc. and Morgan Stanley Capital International, March 2011. All investments involve risk. Foreign securities involve additional risks, including foreign currency changes, political risks, foreign taxes, and different methods of accounting and financial reporting. Past performance is not indicative of future performance. Treasury bills are guaranteed as to repayment of principal and interest by the U.S. government. This information does not constitute a solicitation for sale of any securities. CRSP ranks all NYSE companies by market capitalization and divides them into 10 equally-populated portfolios. AMEX and NASDAQ National Market stocks are then placed into deciles according to their respective capitalizations, determined by the NYSE breakpoints. CRSP Portfolios 1-5 represent large-cap stocks; Portfolios 6-10 represent small-caps; Value is represented by companies with a book-to-market ratio in the top 30% of all companies. Growth is represented by companies with a book-to-market ratio in the bottom 30% of all companies. S&P 500 Index is the Standard & Poor's 500 Index. The S&P 500 Index measures the performance of large-capitalization U.S. stocks. The S&P 500 is an unmanaged market value-weighted index of 500 stocks that are traded on the NYSE, AMEX and NASDAQ. The weightings make each company's influence on the index performance directly proportional to that company's market value. The MSCI EAFE Index (Morgan Stanley Capital International Europe, Australasia, Far East Index) is comprised of over 1,000 companies representing the stock markets of Europe, Australia, New Zealand and the Far East, and is an unmanaged index. EAFE represents non-U.S. large stocks. Foreign securities involve additional risks, including foreign currency changes, political risks, foreign taxes and different methods of accounting and financial reporting. Consumer Price Index (CPI) is a measure of inflation. REITs, represented by the NAREIT Equity REIT Index, is an unmanaged market cap-weighted index comprised of 151 equity REITS. Emerging Markets index represents securities in countries with developing economies and provide potentially high returns. Many Latin American, Eastern European and Asian countries are considered emerging markets. Indexes are unmanaged baskets of securities without the fees and expenses associated with mutual funds and other investments. Investors cannot directly invest in an index.

Based on historical stock market information, returns appear random in the short term. So if you want to own winning assets each year, you can't just invest in one or two asset class categories. Instead, you need to own a variety as to avoid concentration in any one in particular. Some of these asset classes may be performing well at a given time, while others will be lagging. That's how the market works.

During the financial crisis and market meltdown of 2008, if you had been invested in just one asset class such as the S&P 500, your net worth may have been down about 37%. However, if you diversified and built a portfolio that included bonds and T-bills, asset classes which both experienced positive returns in 2008, you would have been in better shape.

In fact, the benefits of diversification are often most evident during bear markets. Exhibit 7.2 illustrates the growth of stocks versus a diversified portfolio during two of the worst performance periods in recent history.

The blue line illustrates the hypothetical growth of $1,000 invested in stocks during the mid-1970s recession and the 2007–2009 bear market. The gray line illustrates the hypothetical growth of $1,000 invested in a diversified portfolio of 35% stocks, 40% bonds, and 25% Treasury bills during these same two periods.

Over the course of both time periods, the diversified portfolio lost less than the pure stock portfolio.

Exhibit 7.2: **Diversified Portfolios in Various Market Conditions**
Performance during and after select bear markets

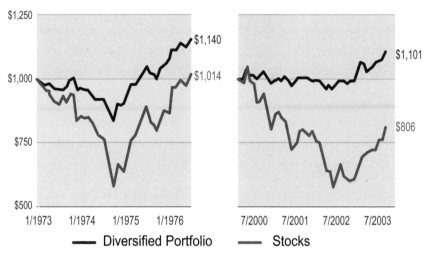

— Diversified Portfolio   — Stocks

Past performance is no guarantee of future results. Diversified portfolio: 35% stocks, 40% bonds, 25% Treasury bills. Hypothetical value of $1,000 invested at beginning of January 1973 and November 2007, respectively. This is for illustrative purposes only and not indicative of any investment. An investment cannot be made directly in an index. Stocks in this example are represented by the Standard & Poor's 500®, an unmanaged group of securities considered to be representative of the stock market in general. Bonds are represented by the 20-year U.S. Government Bond, and Treasury bills by the 30-day U.S. Treasury bill. The data assumes reinvestment of income and does not account for taxes or transaction costs. © 2010 Morningstar. All Rights Reserved. 3/1/2010.

Think about the potential benefits of diversification this way. Say you're packing to go on an extensive road trip across the country. Along the way you plan to hit some Florida beaches, so you pack sunscreen. You also will visit relatives in New England, so you pack some sweaters in case it's cold. In addition, your travels will take you to the Pacific Northwest, so you make sure to include an umbrella. By being prepared for the wide variety of conditions you're likely to experience during your long trip, you'll reduce the risk of having negative moments and maximize your probability of enjoying your experiences no matter where you are along the way.

Investing can also be compared to a journey. As an investor, you're going to experience some days that are sunny and warm and others that are stormy and cold. Conditions will sometimes change unexpectedly and with great force, while other times you'll enjoy long stretches of consistent weather. Knowing that, you'd need to ask yourself: How will I pack for this trip so that I maximize my chances of having a great experience and minimize the risk of having a really bad time?

Diversification is the key to packing wisely for an investment journey. It helps make you better prepared to deal with the various experiences you'll have along the way.

Investors tend to understand that diversification can reduce the overall amount of volatility in an investment portfolio. If your portfolio consists entirely of one stock — a financial services company, for example — your level of wealth is dependent entirely on the value of that stock. If the company experiences a significant setback or goes out of business, your wealth can be destroyed. Consider, for example, if all or even the majority of your portfolio was invested in Lehman Brothers stock or Wachovia or GM or AIG or any of the other companies that ran into severe troubles during the "Great Recession."

But adding another stock to that portfolio immediately reduces the risk that a blow-up at the first company will destroy your wealth. If that second stock is from an entirely different industry — technology, let's say — whose health and stability are affected by different factors, that risk may fall even further. If you then add a third stock from an entirely different area of the market — an oil company in a small overseas market, let's say — you cut your risk further still. Repeat this process thousands of times and you have the basis for a diversified stock portfolio in which no one company, industry or country has a disproportionate ability to damage your wealth. Then by adding other types of assets beyond equities — such as bonds or REITs, for example — you can further enhance your diversification and cut down on risk even more.

The end result: The losses you'll experience when some asset classes perform poorly may be somewhat (or entirely) offset by gains from other asset classes that are doing well.

This approach is what we refer to as "diversifying with structure" — using academic and economic research, such as Fama and French's research on equities and small and value stocks, to build a broadly diversified portfolio that tries to maximize return for your chosen level of risk.

If you own many different asset classes and many different individual securities within those asset classes, you don't have to worry as much if one or even many of those investments don't pan out — you have a whole host of other investments to help make up for the losers. And your portfolio likely won't experience the extreme, nerve-wracking swings in value that a highly concentrated portfolio would. The less worried you are about your portfolio and the less volatile it is from year to year, the less likely you'll be to panic during market downturns and make poor decisions — like selling out of stocks right at a market bottom — that could damage your financial future.

There's another potential benefit to diversification that is just as powerful yet less appreciated: lowering volatility has a potential impact on returns.

For illustration purposes only, consider exhibit 7.3, which shows two $100,000 portfolios. Each one has an average monthly return of 1 percent. But note that Investment A's return each month swings dramatically between +10 percent and -8 percent. By contrast, Investment B is much less volatile. Its monthly return alternates between just +4 percent and -2 percent. Even though both investments produce the same monthly return, the lower volatility Investment B generates much more growth over time. An investor in volatile Investment A would have ended up with much less wealth over three decades — some $2.2 million less, in fact. In stark contrast, an investor in the less volatile Investment B would have done a much better job protecting and growing his or her wealth.

Exhibit 7.3: **The Potential Impact of Volatility on a $100,000 Portfolio**

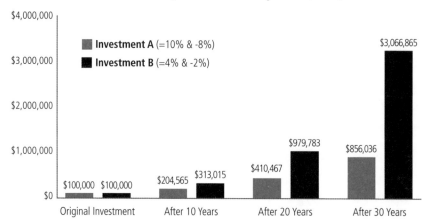

Source: Loring Ward. For illustrative purposes only. Each investment has an average monthly return of 1%, but very different volatility profiles. Investment A (higher volatility) achieves the 1% return by alternating monthly between 10% and –8%, while Investment B (lower volatility) achieves the same average return by alternating between 4% and –2%. The table shows the value of an initial investment of $100,000 with no additions or withdrawals invested over 10, 20 and 30 years. Investment A and B are not representative of a real investment, i.e., no dividends are paid and there are no management fees deducted.

Is Diversification On The Ropes?

It's important to recognize that while diversifying with structure can help reduce a portfolio's overall volatility and increase its potential returns, it cannot guarantee that you won't lose money. This is especially true when there are huge shocks to global markets and economies — such as the worldwide credit crisis that resulted from the blow-up in subprime mortgages in 2008. The depth and breadth of these problems shook the global financial system to its core and left investors with very few places to hide.

In that environment, asset classes that would normally react differently to an event tended to move together. For example, most major equity categories — large-cap stocks, small-cap stocks, large-cap foreign shares and emerging markets equities — all fell by 30% or more. Holding a mix of various types of stocks did investors little good that year — a situation that prompted some investors and investment gurus to declare that diversification was dead.

However, we believe that diversification is as alive and well as ever. One common misconception about diversification is that as one market or asset class goes down, another invariably goes up — for example, when the U.S. market falls, overseas markets rise. Such an offset is more than we can reasonably expect from diversification.

To see why, it's necessary to understand the concept of correlation. Correlation represents the relationship between asset classes during an investment cycle. If two asset classes have a correlation of +1, their values will move simultaneously in the same direction. If the two asset classes have a correlation of -1, their prices will move in opposite directions. Combining asset classes with low correlations therefore can give your portfolio a smoother ride over time. By contrast, owning various asset classes with high correlations gives you less overall diversification.

Many people assume that the correlation between different asset classes is completely negative and that their prices move in opposite directions. In fact, nearly all correlations between investments are positive to some degree. As seen in Exhibit 7.4, U.S. and international stocks have a correlation of +0.886 — meaning that international stocks are likely to post gains when the U.S. market is rising, and post losses when the U.S. market is falling. But note that the correlation between U.S. and international stocks is not a perfect correlation of +1. This means that the magnitude of the gains and losses will be different. Indeed, that's exactly what we saw during the recent bear market. The S&P 500 plunged 37% in 2008, while international stocks did even worse — falling 43%.

From a diversification standpoint, an investor who held both U.S. and foreign stocks would have done better — less bad, really — than an investor who was heavily concentrated in international stocks and had little or no domestic exposure. Both investors obviously would have suffered big losses. But the diversified investor would have a smaller hole to climb out of.

The upshot: Diversification isn't dependent on negative correlations. Obviously, combining two negatively correlated assets is highly desirable. For example, U.S. small-cap stocks (as represented by the CRSP Deciles 6-10 in Exhibit 7.4) have a -0.21 correlation with five-year U.S. Treasury notes. That means when small-cap stock prices rise, prices of five-year Treasuries should fall (and vice versa). However, even asset classes with positive correlations will experience differences in the magnitude of their gains and losses. What's more, their various rates of recovery will likely be different.

Exhibit 7.4: **Correlation of Various Asset Classes**

Data Series	One-Month US Treasury Bills	Five-Year US Treasury Notes	CRSP Deciles 1-10 Index (market)	Fama/French US Large Value Index (ex utilities)	CRSP Deciles 6-10 Index	Fama/French International Value Index	Dimensional International Small Cap Index	Dimensional Emerging Markets Index	Dow Jones Wilshire REIT Index (Full Cap)
One-Month US Treasury Bills	1.00								
Five-Year US Treasury Notes	0.14	1.00							
CRSP Deciles 1-10 Index (market)	0.06	-0.12	1.00						
Fama/French US Large Value Index (ex utilities)	0.09	-0.13	0.82	1.00					
CRSP Deciles 6-10 Index	-0.03	-0.21	0.83	0.65	1.00				
Fama/French International Value Index	-0.09	-0.14	0.65	0.66	0.56	1.00			
Dimensional International Small-Cap Index	-0.23	-0.19	0.57	0.47	0.64	0.85	1.00		
Dimensional Emerging Markets Index	-0.15	-0.21	0.71	0.60	0.72	0.65	0.67	1.00	
Dow Jones Wilshire REIT Index (Full Cap)	-0.05	0.01	0.29	0.34	0.38	0.29	0.24	0.30	1.00

Source: Dimensional Fund Advisors

Structural Diversification

To enjoy the potential benefits that diversification offers, you need to diversify structurally and intelligently. Simply buying a bunch of stocks, bonds, mutual funds or other investments doesn't automatically mean that you have dampened your portfolio's risk and enhanced its potential return. Structural diversification requires you to be thoughtful and systematic in your approach to building and maintaining your portfolio.

Too often, however, investors tend to simply collect investments. They buy a stock because they heard it was hot or because their uncle works for the firm, or they invest in several funds that they read about in various magazines without regard for whether those funds complement each other.

For example, say you own an index mutual fund that attempts to track the performance of the S&P 500 and you decide to add to your portfolio an ETF that tracks the Dow Jones Industrial Average. That move doesn't add any meaningful diversification benefits because both of those investments hold shares of domestic, large-company stocks. Therefore, those two investments should react similarly to new developments in the markets and the economy. When domestic large-cap stocks are down, both of your investments should decline — and probably by roughly the same amount, since their holdings are so similar. As a result, there's nothing in your portfolio to help dampen the impact of those losses on your wealth.

To avoid that type of scenario, investors need to stop simply collecting investments for random reasons and instead own assets that are designed to work together to create portfolios that are stronger than their individual component pieces. That means holding asset classes and investments that have dissimilar price movements from each other and don't react the same way to new developments — in other words, asset classes with relatively low correlations that can "zig" when others "zag." Here's how:

1. Diversify among large- and small-cap stocks. We've seen that small-cap stocks have tended to outperform large-cap shares over time. But that journey has not been a consistently smooth one. As shown in Exhibit 7.5, large-caps and small-caps tend to take turns leading the performance race. What's more, small-caps can lag large-caps for years (and vice versa). For example, large-cap stocks gained 16.5% annually from 1984 through 1991, while small-caps gained just 9.5% a year on average during that time. Even if you are a firm believer in the advantages of small-caps, could you stick with an entirely small-cap portfolio as you watched it lag for eight years? For the vast majority of investors, the answer is a resounding "no." Likewise, large-caps can experience years of poor performance — as they did from 1975 through 1982, returning 14.9% annually while small-caps soared 31.7%. Therefore, it may make sense to include both large- and small-cap stocks in the equity portion of your portfolio. However, given the long-term historical outperformance of small stocks, we do believe in overweighting small vs. large.

Exhibit 7.5: **Small-Caps Versus Large-Caps Over Various Time Periods**

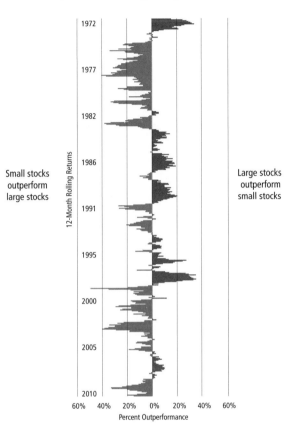

Source: Dimensional Fund Advisors. Large-cap stocks are represented by the Standard & Poor's 500 Index, an unmanaged market value-weighted index of 500 large company stocks that are traded on the NYSE, AMEX and NASDAQ. The Center for Research in Security Prices (CRSP) ranks all NYSE companies by market capitalization and divides them into 10 equally-populated portfolios. AMEX and NASDAQ National Market stocks are then placed into deciles according to their respective capitalizations, determined by the NYSE breakpoints. CRSP Portfolios 6-10 represent small caps.

2. Diversify among value and growth stocks. We saw in the last chapter that value stocks have historically outperformed growth shares over time. But just like small- and large-caps, value and growth stocks each go in and out of favor over various time periods — and each has a habit of going on extended runs at the expense of the other (see Exhibit 7.6).

While growth stocks as a group handily beat value shares in aggregate from 1995 through 1999 (31.2% versus 21.9%, respectively), value won from 1972 through 1989 — gaining 16.6% versus 9.8% for growth. Again, given the long-term historical outperformance of value stocks, we do believe in overweighting value vs. growth.

Exhibit 7.6: **Growth Versus Value Over Various Time Periods**

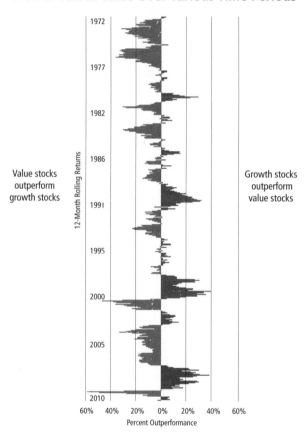

Source: Dimensional Fund Advisors. The Center for Research in Security Prices (CRSP) ranks all NYSE companies by market capitalization and divides them into 10 equally-populated portfolios. AMEX and NASDAQ National Market stocks are then placed into deciles according to their respective capitalizations, determined by the NYSE breakpoints. Value is represented by companies with a book-to-market ratio in the top 30% of all companies. Growth is represented by companies with a book-to-market ratio in the bottom 30% of all companies.

3. Bring international stocks into the mix. Events that affect U.S. companies don't always have the same impact on firms in foreign countries. As a result, shares of overseas companies may rise when the overall domestic market is slumping. This is especially true with emerging markets stocks — shares of firms in developing nations such as Brazil and Thailand that have different economic drivers behind their growth than the U.S. (see Exhibit 7.7). For example, emerging markets stock returned 29 percent in 2005 — a year when the U.S. market gained just 4.9 percent.

Exhibit 7.7: **Emerging Markets Stocks Versus U.S. Stocks Over Various Time Periods**

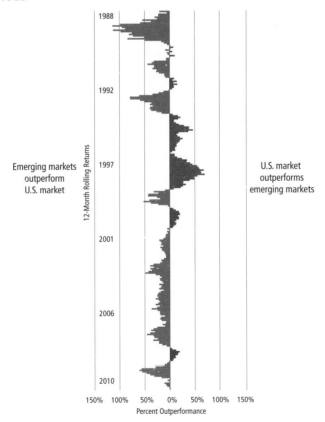

Source: Dimensional Fund Advisors. Investing in foreign securities may involve certain additional risks, including exchange rate fluctuations, less liquidity, greater volatility, different financial and accounting standards and political instability.

There's another reason to diversify internationally: Currently, more than 50% of the global stock market's value comes from non-U.S. companies. Therefore, investors who forsake foreign investments don't own many of the world's most well known and successful companies — including Sony, Nokia, Honda and Royal Dutch Shell. By adding international stocks to the mix, investors can not only better diversify their portfolios but also give themselves more opportunities to profit from the growth of capitalism across the globe.

4. Add short-term, high-quality bonds to reduce risk. Bonds are a crucial asset class for many investors, as only the more aggressive among us are comfortable owning portfolios made up entirely of stocks. Bond prices are much less volatile than stock prices and they often move in the opposite direction of stocks, making bonds an excellent potential source of diversification and risk reduction that can help protect wealth when stocks suffer. Most recently, we saw this during the market meltdown of 2008. As stocks plummeted by 37% or more, intermediate-term U.S. government bonds rose by 13%.

We believe the most effective way to diversify a stock portfolio with bonds is to allocate a percentage of your portfolio to high-quality, short-term fixed-income investments. Why those investments, specifically? Because bonds with longer maturities and of lower quality entail more risk than do short-term bonds of very high quality. Bonds that mature farther in the future are hit harder by unexpected increases in interest rates, while bonds with lower credit quality have a higher risk of default.

Unfortunately, these additional risks don't typically provide adequate compensation to investors who take them. Note in Exhibit 7.8 that the risk (as measured by standard deviation) of 20-year bonds is much greater than the risk in Treasury securities with maturities of just one year or less. Now notice how similar the historical returns in each category are. Clearly, owning relatively volatile long-term bonds doesn't offer much in the way of extra returns over extremely low-risk short-term issues. Likewise, as seen in Exhibit 7.9, bonds with lower credit ratings (such as BBB and high-yield bonds) do not tend to offer ample enough return potential over higher quality bonds to justify their additional risk.

Exhibit 7.8: The Risk/Return Trade-Off in Fixed-Income — Long-Term vs. Short-Term Bonds

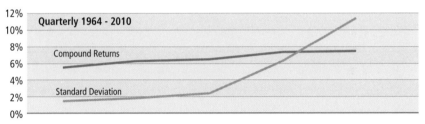

Maturity	One-Month U.S. Treasury Bills	BofA Merrill Lynch Six-Month U.S. Treasury Bills	BofA Merrill Lynch One-Year U.S. Treasury Notes	Five-Year U.S. Treasury Notes	Long-Term Government Bonds
Compound Return (%)	5.45	6.20	6.41	7.27	7.37
Standard Deviation (%)	1.42	1.77	2.34	6.21	11.30

Source: One-Month US Treasury Bills, Five-Year US Treasury Notes, and Twenty-Year (Long-Term) US Government Bonds provided by Ibbotson Associates. Six-Month US Treasury Bills provided by CRSP (1964-1977) and B of A Merrill Lynch (1978-present). One-Year US Treasury Notes provided by CRSP (1964-May 1991) and B of A Merrill Lynch (June 1991-present). Ibbotson data © Stocks, Bonds, Bills, and Inflation Yearbook™, Ibbotson Associates, Chicago (annually updated work by Roger G. Ibbotson and Rex A. Sinquefield). CRSP data provided by the Center for Research in Security Prices, University of Chicago. The Merrill Lynch Indices are used with permission; copyright 2011 B of A Merrill Lynch, Pierce, Fenner & Smith Incorporated; all rights reserved. Assumes reinvestment of dividends. Past performance is not indicative of future results. Standard deviation annualized from quarterly data. Standard deviation is a statistical measurement of how far the return of a security (or index) moves above or below its average value. The greater the standard deviation, the riskier an investment is considered to be.

Exhibit 7.9: **The Risk/Return Trade-Off in Fixed-Income —
High Quality vs. Lower Quality Bonds**

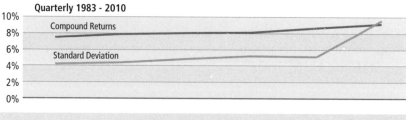

Quality	Government	AAA	AA	A	BBB	High Yield
Compound Return (%)	7.40	7.80	7.95	8.03	8.58	9.07
Standard Deviation (%)	4.16	4.33	4.77	5.13	5.06	9.49

Source: Government rating is Barclays Capital US Government Bond Index Intermediate, AAA rating is Barclays Capital US Intermediate Credit Aaa Index. AA rating is Barclays Capital US Intermediate Credit Aa Index. A rating is Barclays Capital US Intermediate Credit A Index. BBB rating is Barclays Capital US Intermediate Credit BBB Index. High Yield rating is Barclays High Yield Composite Bond Index Intermediate. Indices are not available for direct investment. Assumes reinvestment of dividends. Past performance is not indicative of future results. Standard deviation annualized from quarterly data. Standard deviation is a statistical measurement of how far the return of a security (or index) moves above or below its average value. The greater the standard deviation, the riskier an investment is considered to be.

There are two key lessons here. One is that short-term, high-quality fixed-income investments should do a much better job at dampening the volatility of an overall portfolio than other types of bonds because their prices are more stable. That stability can help to reduce a portfolio's amount of price fluctuation. The other is that you may want to think twice before seeking to generate lots of additional return by owning long-term, low-quality bonds that require you to take on significant risk for not much reward.

We hope by now that it's become clear that diversifying your portfolio is not just a smart move but can even be a liberating experience. Diversifying means that you no longer have to go through the futile and oftentimes fruitless effort of trying to predict the future and make the right moves all the time. Instead you can spend your time on your business, your family or yourself — instead of trying buy and sell the "right" investments.

CHAPTER 8

Building and Implementing Your Investment Portfolio

The next step in the *Structured Wealth Management* investment consulting process is to create a portfolio based on your particular situation and then implement it using specific investment vehicles. As you'll see in this chapter, it's also important to place those investment vehicles in the appropriate types of accounts, as well as formally document your portfolio choices and the reasons behind them by implementing an Investment Policy Statement.

Key Questions to Consider When Building Your Portfolio

To begin, you need to consider a series of issues that will help you build the right portfolio for you — one that intends to take into account your specific goals, time horizon, liquidity needs and your views on investment risk. These issues will help ensure that your portfolio provides you with the appropriate trade-off between risk and return so that you can stick with your plan during a variety of market cycles and let your portfolio do its most important job: working to get you to your biggest financial goals.

Broadly, the issues to consider are divided into three main areas: risk capacity, risk tolerance and investment preferences.

Risk Capacity Considerations

Your capacity to bear investment risk on a purely objective basis will be determined by factors such as:

- **Your portfolio goals.** Nearly all investors have one of five primary goals: retirement funding, education funding, wealth accumulation, capital preservation, or estate maximization. Of course, you may have more than one of these goals — for example, funding a comfortable retirement for yourself and your spouse while also passing on a significant portion of your estate to children and grandchildren. Therefore, you might choose to create multiple portfolios, each one designed to achieve a specific objective.

- **Your time horizon.** You must determine the approximate length of time that your money will need to be invested in order to determine an appropriate allocation to stocks in your portfolio. Because equities can generate substantial losses over the short-term — the worst-ever one-year loss for the S&P 500 index was -37 percent (see Exhibit 8.1) — it is usually inappropriate to invest in equities for any goal with a time horizon of five years or fewer. Generally, however, portfolios with longer-term goals have a higher capacity for stock market risk. The reason: Stock returns fluctuate less and less the longer you hold equities. Indeed, as seen in Exhibit 8.1, stocks have generated positive returns during 100% of rolling 15-year periods since 1972.

Exhibit 8.1: **The Range of Stock Market Returns Over Various Time Periods** — S&P 500 Index Rolling Returns 1972 - 2010

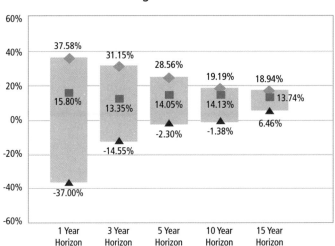

The chart above shows the maximum, median and minimum returns for the S&P 500 index over 12-month rolling periods since 1972. Source: Standard & Poor's. Past performance is no guarantee of future results, and values fluctuate. Principal value, share prices and investment returns fluctuate with changes in market conditions, so that an investor's shares when redeemed or sold, may be worth more or less than their original cost.

- **Your income and liquidity requirements.** Another key factor in determining the right asset allocation is your need for current income from the portfolio. What is your current income requirement from your portfolio this year per $100,000 invested: 0-1 percent, 1-2 percent, 2-3 percent, 3-4 percent, 4-5 percent or more than 6 percent? In addition, consider if you will require a significant withdrawal of principal from the portfolio within the next five years to fund a major expense — such as buying a home or paying for college tuition. If that's the case, how big a withdrawal from your portfolio will you need to take, per $100,000 invested: 1-10%, 10-20%, 20-40%, 40-60%, or more? As a rule of thumb, you should have enough money invested in relatively stable short-term, high-quality fixed-income investments to meet three to five years' worth of liquidity and income needs.

Risk Tolerance Considerations

To create the right portfolio for your situation, you also need to consider questions that go beyond your objective ability to incur investment risk and help you assess your emotional comfort with risk. The reason: If you cannot psychologically withstand the amount of risk in your portfolio, you may be tempted to deviate from your investment plan during periods of extreme market behavior — for example, selling out of stocks during deep bear markets and missing the benefits of future stock market rallies. The capacity to take on risk based on your goals and time horizon won't do you much good if you panic when the markets tumble and make rash changes to your portfolio that could throw off your entire financial plan.

To help you get a better handle on your tolerance to accept risk, consider issues such as:

- **Your general comfort level with risk.** Do you try to avoid risk as much as possible in your life, including in non-financial areas? Would you describe yourself more as cautious or willing to take some calculated risks? Or are you generally a risk taker?

- **Your feelings about market fluctuations.** Think about watching the ups and downs in your portfolio — especially back in 2008 and early 2009 when the market was rising and falling by hundreds of points on a given day. When you think about those wild swings, do you say to yourself, "I can accept lots of ups and down so I can maximize returns?" Or are you more likely to be willing to tolerate *some* fluctuations in the value of your portfolio in order to keep pace with inflation? Or would you rather not experience *any* fluctuations even if that means accepting lower returns that don't keep up with inflation?

- **Your reaction to market declines on your portfolio's value.** Let's say you have a portfolio worth $1 million, and a bear market causes the value of that portfolio to plummet by $300,000 over the course of a 12-month period. If you looked at your account statement and saw that your portfolio was now worth just $700,000, what would you do? Can you confidently say that you would not sell? Would you be uncertain about what to do next? Would you almost certainly sell after experiencing such a large loss in just one year? Or would you never even have invested in a portfolio that could lose so much money so quickly in the first place?

Investment Preferences

Finally, given what you've learned about the diversification benefits and risk/return characteristics of international investments, value-oriented stocks and small-company stocks in previous chapters, how comfortable are you with owning each of these three types of investments in your portfolio — very uncomfortable, somewhat uncomfortable, somewhat comfortable, comfortable or very comfortable?

Establishing your investment preferences in these areas will enable you to better decide if you want to tilt your portfolio toward those asset classes that have shown to reward investors over time — and if so, determine an allocation strategy that will help you realize your most important goals.

Implementing Your Portfolio Strategy

Investors today have more options than ever in terms of investment vehicles and products. Despite the increasing number of choices that exist, we believe that mutual funds are an excellent solution for the vast majority of investors looking to achieve their long-term goals. The major benefits of mutual funds include:

- **Diversification.** Mutual funds typically hold huge numbers of stocks and bonds — upwards of 500 in some cases — from numerous industries, and may even invest in multiple countries from around the globe. In other words, funds can provide instant diversification at a much lower cost than if you tried to create your own diversified portfolio of thousands of stocks, bonds and other investments.

- **Regulations.** Mutual funds are one of the most highly regulated investment vehicles. It is noteworthy that many of the failed Ponzi schemes and frauds that were uncovered during the Great Recession (Madoff, Stanford, Phillip Barry) were in investment products other than mutual funds.

Unlike unregistered investment products, a mutual fund is one of the most highly regulated investment products.

- The mutual fund itself is registered with the SEC as an investment company under the Investment Company Act of 1940.

- A mutual fund can only be advised by an investment advisor registered with the SEC pursuant to the Investment Advisors Act of 1940.

- The shares of a mutual fund are generally securities themselves registered with the SEC pursuant to the Securities Act of 1933 and regulated per the Securities and Exchange Act of 1934.

Also, mutual funds have ticker symbols through which valuations can be determined quickly and easily, either by calling a financial advisor, typing in the ticker into a financial website, or looking in a newspaper. More complex securities, like mortgage-backed securities, derivatives, and private placements are not always easy to evaluate and price and therefore can be sources of abuse.

Active Versus Passive

Among fund options, there are passive funds and active funds. Passive funds attempt to match the performance of an entire asset class or a particular index that represents an asset class. Active funds attempt to beat the performance of an asset class or index by actively buying and selling securities. If you've read this far, you no doubt can guess that we believe the best option for investors is to use passive funds that do not attempt to pick winners, avoid losers or jump in and out of the market at the most opportune times. As we've illustrated, investors who take those actions fail the vast majority of the time and therefore this methodology does not seem a prudent way of investing for the future.

Passive funds also offer the key benefit of style consistency. If you create an overall structure for your portfolio — an asset allocation strategy — you need the investments you use to stay committed to their respective investment styles. You don't want a fund that is in stocks one day, cash the next. This makes maintaining a suitable asset allocation very difficult. For that reason, active funds aren't always appropriate for investors who wish to build and maintain well thought out, diversified asset allocation strategies that require consistency.

Finally, passive funds typically have much lower costs and management fees than active funds. That's because passive funds simply own all the stocks that make up their target index or asset class. They don't have to spend lots of time, money and human resources trying to identify the winners and losers and making numerous trades that generate costs — costs that get passed on to their shareholders. The difference between the costs of the average actively managed mutual fund and those of the average passively managed fund can be substantial. As you can see from Exhibit 8.2, this cost differential in 2009 was 1.54%. That's a big difference to pay someone, when the odds are that they may not be able to outperform the passive managers over the long-term.

Exhibit 8.2: **Average Mutual Fund Costs in 2009**

Funds	Annual Reported Net Expense Ratio	SAI Charges*	Total Fees
Average Actively Managed Mutual Fund	1.14%	1.53%	2.67%
Average Passively Managed Mutual Fund	0.52%	0.61%	1.13%

*Statement of Additional Information (SAI). Based on Turnover Ratio % times average SAI of 1.47%.

The illustration results are only an estimate and do not reflect advisory fees charged by your investment advisor. Source: Lipper Data as of December 31, 2009

Among passive funds, there are three main options to consider:

- **Index funds.** As you're probably aware, index funds attempt to replicate the performance of specific commercial indices (the S&P 500, the Russell 2000, the MSCI EAFE, etc.). They offer investors an easy way to gain exposure to a broad range of investment categories and styles. The downside to index funds is that, because the funds need to track their indices as closely as possible, their managers must buy and sell certain stocks whenever their target index deletes or adds securities. Such trading can generate unwanted costs.

- **Exchange traded funds.** An ETF is similar to an index fund in that it seeks to mirror the holdings of a commercial index and match its performance. Because of how they're structured, however, ETFs have expenses that are often even lower than those of traditional index mutual funds. They also offer a high degree of tax efficiency. An enormous number of ETFs exist, allowing investors to build broadly diversified passive portfolios with exposure to a wide variety of investments.

- **Asset class funds.** Less well known among investors than index funds or ETFs, asset class funds — as the name suggests — attempt to deliver the investment returns of an entire broad asset class. In that respect they are extremely similar to index funds and ETFs. But unlike those two options, asset class funds don't necessarily own the exact same securities that are found in a commercial index like the S&P 500. Instead, they hold large numbers of securities with similar risk and expected return characteristics. A small-cap stock asset class fund, for example, might define small-caps somewhat differently than would an index fund or ETF that tracks the Russell 2000 index of small-company stocks. Asset class fund investors believe that these funds offer truer and more accurate exposure to various segments of the financial market.

A Word About Asset Location

Once you've created your ideal portfolio strategy and implemented your plan using specific investment vehicles, you still have another important duty: Deciding how to best locate your assets in your portfolio.

Asset location is all about placing each of your various investments into one of two types of accounts — taxable or non-taxable/tax-deferred — to achieve optimal tax efficiency, defer taxes and generate the best after-tax returns possible. The best location for your assets depends on factors such as the tax laws at the time, the tax and return characteristics of the securities you own, your income tax bracket, and your need for liquidity.

There are some general guidelines that you can use to start thinking about which of your investments are best-suited to each type of account. For example, low-cost index funds, ETFs and asset class funds that don't make a lot of trades and are already highly tax efficient — as well as investments like tax-free municipal bonds — are often placed in taxable accounts, because placing them in tax-advantaged accounts doesn't add much benefit in terms of minimizing taxes. But investments that generate significant taxable income — such as some taxable bond funds and real estate investment trusts (REITs) funds

— are often placed in tax-deferred or non-taxable accounts to help mitigate current tax liabilities. There is no one "right" answer when it comes to asset location. Your specific needs, circumstances and tax situation should drive the decision.

Put It in Writing

The final step in this part of the *Structured Wealth Management* investment consulting process is to create an Investment Policy Statement. This is a written document spelling out the key components of your financial situation and investment plan, and the reasons behind why you have structured your portfolio the way you have. It should contain your answers to the types of questions outlined earlier in this chapter — answers regarding your goals, time horizon, risk tolerance and ability to withstand risk, liquidity and income requirements, and your approach to your portfolio's asset allocation and investment vehicles.

By putting this information in writing, you'll clarify what goals you are hoping to achieve by investing and why you have chosen to use the approach you are using. Such clarity can be extremely beneficial to you — both when markets are soaring and possibly tempting you to chase hot market sectors and also when markets are plummeting and perhaps tempting you to cash out of stocks and deviate from your plan. An Investment Policy Statement can help you avoid the worst and most dangerous emotional reactions to various market developments — a topic we'll tackle in detail in the next chapter. For that reason, we strongly encourage that you create an Investment Policy Statement that you can refer to whenever you think it's time to make big changes to your portfolio or overall saving and investing strategy. It may be one of the most valuable documents you'll ever use.

CHAPTER 9

Invest for the Long Term

By creating and implementing a portfolio strategy customized around your needs and situation, you've put yourself on a sound path toward achieving your investment goals. However, your job isn't finished. In fact, you now must contend with perhaps the biggest challenge you'll ever face as an investor: avoiding the foolish mistakes that can jeopardize your financial future.

As investors — and as human beings, really — we are predisposed to constantly take action. We're always racing around trying to "get ahead of the curve." It's counterintuitive in our culture to believe that doing nothing is in any way a better idea than doing something.

And yet, when it comes to investing, being overactive is the downfall of too many investors. That's why one of the smartest moves you can make is to be patient and disciplined regarding your portfolio and your wealth management plan. Being patient and disciplined and investing for the long term means doing less, not more. It means exercising restraint instead of charging ahead. And it means staying focused on what is truly important to your life goals and ignoring the enormous amount of emotion and "noise" that too often clouds investors' judgment and prompts them to make rash moves that hurt their chances of achieving all that is important to them.

As you'll see in this chapter, a long-term perspective is a key driver of investment success. But it's also a task that can be extraordinarily difficult to achieve because of our hard-wired tendencies. The good news: There are steps you can take that will help you be a more patient and disciplined investor — one who is in the best position to reach your long-term goals with the least amount of effort and stress possible.

The Importance of Staying Invested

Once you've built your portfolio and are invested the way you want to be, it's critical to stick with your plan and not jump in and out of various investments and asset classes. The reason: Deviating from your disciplined approach by being out of a particular market segment can decimate your portfolio's long-term returns.

Consider Exhibit 9.1, which shows the performance of the S&P 500 from 1970 through 2009. The index during that entire 40-year period generated an annualized compound return of 9.8 percent. If you owned an index or asset class fund that tracked the S&P 500 and matched its returns over that entire period, you would have earned the same return (minus expenses).

If, however, you traded actively and moved in and out of the fund, your returns would most likely have suffered. By missing just the single best day for the S&P 500 during those 40 years — that's one day out of 40 years — your annualized return would have fallen to 9.6 percent. And if you had missed the best 15 days over that entire period, you would have earned a mere 3.7 percent on your investment — less than you would have made by investing in Treasury bills. Put in dollar terms, the difference is even more startling. If you'd stayed in the market for the whole period, your $100,000 would have grown to $4,961,400. Missing the best 10 days in that period would have cut your returns almost in half to $2,186,801. This more than $2 million dollar difference is a stark illustration of the dangers of trying to time the markets.

Exhibit 9.1: **The Effect of Missing the Market's Best Days**

"Time in" vs. "Timing" the Market — Performance of the S&P 500 Index 1970 - 2009

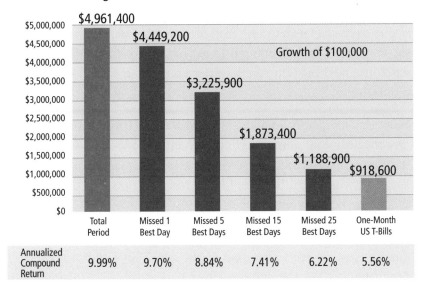

	Total Period	Missed 1 Best Day	Missed 5 Best Days	Missed 15 Best Days	Missed 25 Best Days	One-Month US T-Bills
Annualized Compound Return	9.99%	9.70%	8.84%	7.41%	6.22%	5.56%

Performance data for January 1970-August 2008 provided by CRSP; performance data for September 2008-December 2009 provided by Bloomberg. The S&P data are provided by Standard & Poor's Index Services Group. US bonds and bills data © Stocks, Bonds, Bills, and Inflation Yearbook™, Ibbotson Associates, Chicago (annually updated work by Roger G. Ibbotson and Rex A. Sinquefield).

Indexes are not available for direct investment. Their performance does not reflect the expenses associated with the management of an actual portfolio. Dimensional Fund Advisors is an investment advisor registered with the Securities and Exchange Commission. Information contained herein is compiled from sources believed to be reliable and current, but accuracy should be placed in the context of underlying assumptions. This publication is distributed for educational purposes and should not be considered investment advice or an offer of any security for sale. Past performance is not a guarantee of future results There is always the risk that an investor may lose money.

The upshot: A relatively small number of trading days tends to be responsible for the stock market's strong returns over time. Miss even a handful of those days and you stand to end up with a lot less wealth than you would if you simply stayed "all-in" the entire time.

Of course, it's tempting to think about the flip-side of this situation and wonder what would happen if you avoided the market's very worst days over time. In that case, your returns would look a lot different. However, you've got to ask yourself: Do I feel lucky? Are you agile enough to avoid the market's very worst days year in and year out over several decades? And after you've avoided those down days, are you also astute enough to get back in to the market in time to catch the next big "up" day? To test yourself, answer the following two questions:

- How was my portfolio allocated on October 15th, 2008? On that day, the S&P 500 plummeted 9.0 percent — one of its worst single-day performances in the past 40 years. Did you see that day coming and shift your portfolio out of U.S. stocks to avoid the damage? Or did it hit you unexpectedly?

- How was my portfolio allocated on October 28, 2008? On that date — just 13 days after one of the S&P 500's worst single-day performances — the index delivered one of its best single-day performances, soaring 10.8 percent. Think back. Did you know that was about to happen and therefore get back into stocks or increase your allocation to equities? Or were you, like most other investors, still worried about the possibility of a global financial meltdown and taking a more cautious approach?

If you got it wrong, don't feel bad: You had plenty of company. Investors time and time again get nervous or impatient and break their discipline — typically at exactly the wrong times.

As a result of such ill-timed shifting of money, investors experience substantially lower returns than what the market offers them. For example, while the S&P 500 gained 9.14 percent annually from 1991 through 2010, the average equity fund investor gained just 3.83 percent a year on average — that's a full 5.3 percentage points less than the index (see Exhibit 9.2).

Exhibit 9.2: **Market Rates of Return vs. Investors' Actual Rates of Return**
Average Investor vs. Major Indices 1991 – 2010

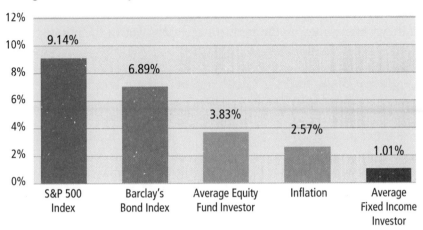

Average stock investor and average bond investor performances were used from a DALBAR study, Quantitative Analysis of Investor Behavior (QAIB), 03/2011. QAIB calculates investor returns as the change in assets after excluding sales, redemptions, and exchanges. This method of calculation captures realized and unrealized capital gains, dividends, interest, trading costs, sales charges, fees, expenses, and any other costs. After calculating investor returns in dollar terms (above), two percentages are calculated: Total investor return rate for the period and annualized investor return rate. Total return rate is determined by calculating the investor return dollars as a percentage of the net of the sales, redemptions, and exchanges for the period. The fact that buy-and-hold has been a successful strategy in the past does not guarantee that it will continue to be successful in the future.

The damage of missing 5.3 percentage points of return a year on average is devastating. A $500,000 investment in a hypothetical mutual fund that earns 9.14 percent annually would grow to roughly $2.94 million in 20 years (not accounting for fees, taxes or expenses). But an investor who earned the typical return of 3.83 percent would have just $1 million — a difference of roughly $1.9 million. Fixed-income investors fared even worse. While the Barclay's bond index gained 6.89 percent annually from 1991 through 2010, the average fixed-income fund investor realized an annualized gain of just 1.01 percent — less than the average rate of inflation during that period.

The upshot: Investors are trading too frequently. They are chasing after hot investments just as those investments are about to go cold. And they are avoiding investments that are positioned to post strong gains. If they weren't, they would perform at least as well as the indices, if not better — and clearly they're not.

Cognitive Biases and the Challenge of Staying Disciplined

There's a good reason why investors tend to consistently make these and other mistakes with their money — mistakes that can cause them to not accumulate nearly as much money as they could. As human beings, we have ingrained tendencies to let our short term emotions guide our longer term decisions, such as investing.

For example, strong emotions can quickly cause us to misinterpret facts and make the wrong moves at the wrong time — repeatedly.

To see how this cycle of emotion plays out in real life, consider Exhibit 9.3. It shows a hypothetical example of what happens to many investors. When the market is on the rise and racking up big gains, investors quickly change from being optimistic to excited to downright elated. They eventually start to worry that they're being left behind by not buying stocks — that their friends are all getting rich and that they better invest heavily in equities in order to look smart and make money. So after spending weeks or even months watching the stock market post strong returns, they buy in or ramp up their allocation to stocks.

Typically what happens is that shortly thereafter the market starts to show signs of weakness and begins to fall. At first, investors might be a bit concerned about these developments, but they find reassurance by telling themselves that "it's only a temporary setback." But it isn't. Stock prices continue to decline and investors become alarmed and frightened — with a growing certainty that "it's different this time" and that stocks have become a sucker's bet that will never pay off. As that fear really kicks in, they sell their stocks or transfer huge chunks of their investment capital money into bonds.

If you paid attention at all during the past few years, you know what typically happens next. Stocks begin to rally once again — often unexpectedly posting outsized gains in a very short window of time.

Exhibit 9.3: The Cycle of Market Emotions

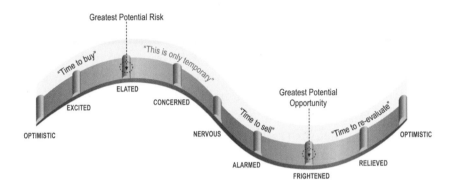

For illustration purposes only

The bottom line for too many investors is that they buy at the top, driven by elation and greed. They then sell out at the bottom and lock in their losses, driven by fear. And they miss the start of the next upswing.

This cycle will no doubt look familiar to many of you. But the question remains: Why do we let our emotions replace our capacity for rational thought and drive our investment decisions in the first place?

The answer lies in a field of academic and economic study called behavioral finance — which studies the many biological and psychological factors that drive our decision-making processes. We like to think of ourselves as fairly rational, but behavioral finance shows otherwise.

Behavioral finance is a fascinating and rapidly evolving field of study. Information about how investors really make decisions is being researched all the time. However, work in this important new field — some of which has won the Nobel Prize in economics — has identified several key ways in which our brains trick us into seeing the investment world one way, when in reality it's something quite different. These cognitive biases include:

- **Anchoring bias.** This reflects our tendency to latch our thinking onto a reference point that we are familiar with — even if that reference point isn't relevant to our particular situation. In an investment context, we tend to "anchor" to the long-term average return of stocks and expect stock returns in any given year to approximate the average. But, of course, stock returns in any given year may be wildly different from the long-term average. This conflicts with our mental "anchor," which causes us to panic when returns are negative in a single year or get extremely exuberant when returns are abnormally high — and make bad investment decisions as a result.

- **Confirmation bias.** This bias occurs when we look only for evidence that confirms our existing beliefs while ignoring or discounting evidence that shows them to be false or questionable. If you think a potential investment is going to be a huge winner, you'll probably seek out other opinions that match yours and believe that people with conflicting beliefs "just don't get it." The investment could be a dog in many ways — but you're not willing to hear it. The result, too often, is a sizeable investment loss. A good historical example of this was in the late 90s high-technology stock boom. Many investors over-allocated their investment capital to high tech stocks, ignoring both their risk profiles and the key principles of diversification. The resulting decline in these technology stocks had a greater effect on investors who had concentrated much of their wealth to this industry.

- **Hindsight bias.** Often we feel that whatever happened was bound to happen — that luck or chance couldn't play a part in a given situation and that ultimately, everything that occurred could have been predicted. If stock prices fall after a long bull run, it must have been because "trees don't grow to the sky" — we knew it all along. But if stock prices continue to rise, it's because "the trend is your friend." Looking back on investments' past performance, it's natural for us to think that we — or someone — should have seen it coming and taken the appropriate action.

For example, think back about the above referenced technology stock bubble back in the late 1990s. With the elapsed time, it's easy for an investor to acknowledge there was a bubble and that stock prices had to plummet. But in the moment, that investor most likely a) didn't see a bubble, b) saw it but didn't do anything to protect himself or c) felt (like so many) that "it's different this time." Hindsight bias often leads to a sense of overconfidence among investors — making them think they're much smarter or adept at picking stocks than they are. Another name for hindsight bias is "Monday morning quarterbacking", named for the tendency for football fans to see so clearly what decisions coaches should have made in the games on Sunday.

By understanding these and other cognitive biases that affect us all, you can do a better a job of recognizing your particular biases and try hard to overcome the tendency to act on your short term emotions. It's not always easy to notice your biases and shut them down, of course. But if you can keep your emotions in check when making investment decisions, you'll find yourself in much better shape down the road.

The Need to Review and Rebalance

Keep in mind that patience and discipline don't mean burying your head in the sand and doing nothing at all. The point is to do only those things that will maximize your chances of having a successful investment experience, and no more.

Take rebalancing. When you review your portfolio's performance, rebalancing should be a key strategy on your list. As financial markets and asset classes rise and fall, your portfolio's exposure to stocks, bonds, cash and other investments will fluctuate as well. Over time, your overall target asset allocations will shift — leaving you with more money invested in stocks than you prefer, for example, and less invested in bonds. The result: You may find that your portfolio now carries more investment risk than you feel comfortable with or need.

Rebalancing is one of the keys to keeping your portfolio on track and maintaining the right balance between growth potential and risk exposure. By rebalancing your portfolio back to its target allocations, you'll better control the level of risk in your portfolio, build more wealth over time, and give yourself a system for shutting down emotional decision making. In fact, you'll be better equipped to consistently do something that all investors say they want to do but rarely accomplish: buy low and sell high.

Rebalancing is a relatively straightforward, easy process to implement. Let's say you have $500,000 invested. Based on your goals and risk profile, you want your portfolio to have a long-term target asset allocation of 60 percent stocks and 40 percent bonds. Initially, $300,000 would be allocated to stocks and $200,000 would be allocated to bonds. If your stock holdings gained 10 percent over the next 12 months and your bond holdings lost 5 percent, your asset allocation would then be 63 percent stocks (worth $330,000) and 37 percent bonds (worth $190,000). To get back to your target 60/40 mix, you would need to sell a portion of your stocks and reallocate the proceeds to your bond holdings.

Two recent periods in market history show the potential advantages of rebalancing back to a target asset mix. In the late 1990s, large-company growth stocks and technology stocks were posting huge gains. An investor using a disciplined approach to rebalancing would have sold some of those stocks as they soared in value and reinvested the proceeds into bonds, in order to keep their desired allocation between stocks and bonds. This would have benefited the investor in two ways: When tech and large-cap stocks began plummeting in 2000, the investor would have avoided some of the worst losses. Additionally, by maintaining his target bond allocation, he would have been well positioned to benefit from the strong gains that bonds began generating as stocks fell.

Also consider the more recent bear market that occurred in 2008 and its effect on a hypothetical static portfolio that is never rebalanced. For example, a portfolio of 50 percent stocks (S&P 500) and 50 percent bonds (five-year Treasury notes) in 1987 would have shifted to an allocation of 73 percent stocks and 27 percent bonds by the end of 2007 — making the portfolio significantly riskier than the original 50/50 portfolio going into one of the worst bear markets for stocks in decades. The return on this more aggressive portfolio would have been a whopping -23.6 percent in 2008. By contrast, the 50/50 portfolio would have declined by just 12 percent — a difference of 11.6 percentage points.

Of course, 2008 wasn't a comfortable time for any investor. But if you had to choose between a regularly rebalanced portfolio with a negative 12 percent return or a portfolio that was never rebalanced and lost nearly 24 percent, chances are you'd be a lot more comfortable with the first option. And as we've seen, your comfort level with and commitment to your investment plan is vitally important. If you can emotionally withstand the ups and downs in your portfolio, you're far less likely to take reckless actions like jumping in and out of the market, or falling victim to some of the cognitive biases highlighted above.

But comfort is only one reason why it makes sense to reduce risk through rebalancing. Lower volatility also means that your portfolio can regain any ground it's lost during bad market environments faster than it could otherwise. For example, say your portfolio declines by 20 percent during a bear market. To get back to where you started, you'd actually need to earn a 25 percent return. And if it fell by 50 percent, you would need a return of 100 percent just to get back to where you stood before that decline.

There's yet another reason why it makes sense to use periodic rebalancing as a way to manage risk: greater overall wealth.

Your rebalancing decisions can be made as part of your overall portfolio review, which should be done on a regular basis such as quarterly, semi-annually or annually (depending on your preferences and the complexity of your portfolio). If, during your review, you see that your portfolio's current allocation to any single asset class is significantly higher than your target allocation to that asset class (say, 3 - 5 percent or more), you might sell some of those assets to realign with your target. Likewise, if you see that your exposure to an asset class is 3-5 percent lower than your target, you might buy more of that investment. By creating strict rebalancing parameters like these, you can more easily overcome the tendency to do what so many investors fail to do time and time again — buy low and sell high.

Your overall portfolio review should also go beyond rebalancing and determine if there have been any major developments in your life or financial situation that necessitate making changes to your overall portfolio. The birth of a child or grandchild, a new job (or loss of an existing job) or other significant life developments can have implications for your investment and wealth management strategies. For example, a new child or grandchild could mean it's time to change the beneficiary designations on your investment accounts, or set up a college savings plan. A new job may mean that you can now increase the amount of money you save toward your long-term goals. It's these types of major developments that should guide your portfolio strategy decisions — not the short-term fluctuations of the markets or your emotional responses to them.

Staying On Track

Being disciplined about our investments is difficult even for the most patient among us. Despite our best intentions, the emotions that rise up in us during extreme market environments can quickly override logic and cause us to make poor decisions with our money. That's why it makes sense to arm yourself with as many tools as possible in order to help you maintain your discipline and stay on track in the face of market volatility.

One such tool is an Investment Policy Statement. As we discussed in chapter 8, your IPS will serve as a written record of your investment strategy and the guidelines you have chosen to follow as an investor. It should spell out all the reasons why you have structured your portfolio as you have, and include details about your chosen approach to rebalancing your portfolio. During every portfolio review, your IPS can remind you of the key facts and tenets of your investment plan — which can help you avoid making short-sighted, emotionally-driven decisions. In addition, many IPS's contain historical high and low returns for various types of portfolios. Such data can be invaluable during a market downturn. For example, say your portfolio is down 20 percent over the past year — a return that could make you panic and sell a big chunk of your investments. However, a review of your IPS might remind you that historically, a portfolio like yours experienced a decline as large as 35 percent over a one-year period. In light of that information, a 20 percent decline could be seen not as an extreme or unlikely event but instead as well within the range of possibility — helping to put the situation in historical perspective and helping you stick with your plan.

A second important resource for investors is a fee-based investment advisor. As the name suggests, fee-based advisors charge clients a fee for their services and are therefore not compensated by commissions on sales of investments. As a result, fee-based advisors' interests are aligned with their clients' interests: The advisors do well only if clients' portfolios do well. That means a fee-based advisor is highly motivated to give you the best advice for your situation at all times — even if that advice is to sit tight and do nothing.

Indeed, one of the biggest ways advisors add value is by bringing discipline to your investing. As we've seen, it's all too easy to let both good and bad events cause us to make changes to our portfolios. Having an advisor to guide you through those ups and downs can help you stay on course and avoid the mistake of breaking your discipline. In that sense, think of an advisor in the same way you might think of a dietician or a personal trainer — as someone who helps you set up a plan, then watches and motivates you to keep doing the right thing so you end up with the results you want. In an advisor's case, you might not lose weight or gain strength — but you might just end up making more money than you would otherwise. Many advisors can bring substantial additional value to your financial life. For example, some may be able to help you with complex tax issues or estate planning needs. Others can integrate these and any other aspect of your finances into one comprehensive solution. In Chapter 12, you'll find information that can help you assess your needs and determine what type of advisor and level of service will suit you best.

CHAPTER 10

Advanced Planning and Trusted Advisory Relationships

As vitally important as the right investment plan is to your financial well-being, it is far from the only thing that matters. In order to fully benefit from *Structured Wealth Management* and maximize your potential for success in all areas of your financial life, you may need to look beyond investments.

That means accurately identifying the key non-investment financial risks you face and then determining the best strategies for mitigating or eliminating those risks. In short, you need to bring Advanced Planning into the mix and make it part of your overall *Structured Wealth Management* plan.

Remember from chapter three that *Structured Wealth Management* consists of three main components: Investment Planning, Advanced Planning and Trusted Advisory Relationships. Since we've covered Investment Planning in depth, we'll now turn to the other two components.

Advanced Planning addresses the entire range of financial needs beyond your portfolio.

Trusted Advisory Relationships involve working effectively with a team of professional advisors (such as attorneys, accountants and advisors) on a regular basis to understand and address your critical needs. These can include: enhancing wealth through tax minimization, transferring wealth to heirs, protecting wealth and supporting charitable causes and non-profit organizations (see Exhibit 10-1).

Exhibit 10-1: **Key Advanced Planning Concerns**

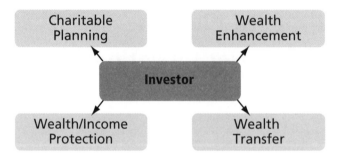

Let's look at how you might develop a smart *Structured Wealth Management* plan for addressing each of these challenges.

Wealth Enhancement

This is the process of maximizing the tax efficiency of current assets and cash flow as well as minimizing fees and unnecessary costs. Key wealth enhancement steps that you should consider implementing as part of a *Structured Wealth Management* plan include the following:

• **Get organized and consolidate accounts.** Before you can maximize the effectiveness of your wealth and do comprehensive Advanced Planning, you need to get a handle on your financial situation. A comprehensive list of all assets and liabilities, as well as income and expenses, should be the starting point for this process. Investors often find that they have numerous investment and bank accounts spread out across multiple fund companies, advisors, banks and brokerage firms. They also might have 401(k) or other retirement accounts from previous jobs, still with their previous employers.

Trimming down the number of accounts you own can help to simplify your financial life and make it easier to manage. Also, by consolidating all of your investment assets with a single firm and meeting a specific minimum, you may be eligible for lower overall pricing on the management of those assets. Likewise, allocating more money to one bank could allow you to earn higher interest rates.

- **Review tax returns.** The importance of having a good CPA should not be overlooked. Your CPA should work with you (and your other advisors) to ensure that they have all relevant financial information in order to accurately project your current tax liability, and avoid underpayment penalties and interest. Additionally, your CPA may recommend alternative strategies that can serve to reduce your taxable income.

- **Assess cash management strategies.** You also might examine the effectiveness of your cash management strategies. Are you earning the maximum amount possible on your short-term cash (consistent with your need for safety and liquidity, of course), or could you put your cash to work more effectively? Many banks and investment firms offer "sweep" accounts that can link up your checking and money market accounts: the majority of your funds are kept in interest earning accounts, with transfers made to your checking accounts as checks are presented for payment.

- **Maximize use of qualified retirement plans and IRAs.** Examine retirement plan options such as IRAs and Roth IRAs to determine their potential as a way to generate tax-deferred or tax-free retirement income. Also, consider converting existing IRA assets to a Roth IRA. This strategy requires tax to be paid at the time of conversion, but eliminates the need to pay taxes as funds are withdrawn. Additionally, there are no required minimum distributions for Roth IRAs, so these funds can continue to grow for the benefit of your heirs.

- **Explore the possible advantage of "wealth shifting."** There are a variety of techniques that can serve as vehicles to transfer wealth from one generation to the next while minimizing both estate and gift taxes. These techniques allow assets that may have a current "low" valuation to be transferred to the next generation in hopes that the valuation increases over time; in this case, you have shifted potential future capital gains out of your estate.

- **Evaluate corporate plans.** Make a point to analyze all executive compensation programs or benefit plans to ensure that they are being maximized on both a tax and benefits basis.

- **Determine ideal asset location.** As we discussed in Chapter 8, owning certain types of assets in taxable accounts and other types in nontaxable or tax-deferred accounts can reduce your tax burden significantly over time. These asset location decisions will come down to factors such as the amount of taxable income an investment tends to generate, your marginal income tax rate, capital gains tax rates and your liquidity needs.

- **Consider your own "investor environment."** For investors who are approaching retirement or already retired, wealth can be enhanced through cost- and tax-cutting measures such as trading down to a smaller home or re-locating to a state with lower taxes.

- **Involve family members where possible.** Review the opportunities in any family-controlled business or investment entities for younger generation family members to "learn on the job" and be compensated as they develop valuable employment skills for the future. Additionally, ensure that the next generation is educated about the fundamentals of wealth and especially about the responsibilities and obligations that come with the transfer of sizable wealth.

Wealth Transfer

Proper estate planning is the most effective way to help ensure that you are able to pass along assets in ways that satisfy your wishes and that provide for the financial health and well-being of your family. It also can reduce or prevent much of the stress that so often occurs when heirs attempt to sort out a family member's estate.

Many people assume that estate planning is applicable only for the very wealthiest among us. This is simply not the case. Even if your net worth is relatively small, you need basic legal documents that give instructions for how you want your assets distributed at your death or if you become incapacitated. Of course, estate planning often gets ignored because it involves considering your own mortality and what will occur after you die (two topics that many of us prefer to avoid). But by asking some tough questions now — How should assets be distributed at death? How and when should heirs receive an inheritance? — you can ensure that your wishes are carried out and that your heirs receive your assets in the most efficient manner.

While tax and investment advice unique to your situation is beyond the scope of this book, there are some key wealth transfer action steps that you may want to consider implementing as part of a *Structured Wealth Management* Plan. We recommend discussing these steps with your financial advisor and other advisors to determine if they make sense for your particular situation.

- **Create/review your will.** Without a will, you face numerous risks that your assets won't go to whom you want — risks that you might not even know exist. If you are married, for example, you might assume that all of your possessions will simply go to your spouse when you die. However, surviving spouses automatically inherit everything in only some states. Additionally, a will allows you to appoint a guardian for your minor children at your death. Without a will, your children will be considered wards of the state, who will decide who will act as guardian. If you already have a will, review it every few years to ensure that it remains relevant and true to your wishes.

- **Review beneficiary designations and asset vestings.** A beneficiary designation on a bank account, life insurance policy, investment account and the like is the ultimate and overriding determinant in how the assets are transferred at death — even if your will or other documents state that the assets should go elsewhere. The upshot: Make sure that your beneficiary designations on all accounts are accurate, up-to-date and reflect your wishes. Additionally, make sure that the vesting of all assets is accurate. For example, if you have created a family trust, make sure that the assets contributed to the trust are re-titled in the trust's name.

- **Create a living will.** This is a document that spells out the specific actions you want (and don't want) taken in regard to your health care in case you can't make such decisions because of illness or incapacity. By creating clarity, such wills can save your family pain, uncertainty and money.

- **Consider various trusts.** One example is a revocable living trust, which can help your assets avoid probate. Avoiding probate saves money and also prevents the details of your estate from becoming public information. You might also consider trusts designed to pass on assets in ways that reduce estate and gift taxes — including irrevocable life insurance trusts and qualified terminable interest property trusts. These more complex trust options require the help of an estate planning attorney who can set up the trusts in accordance with all applicable laws.

- **Review life insurance opportunities.** Ownership of life insurance policies by a trust or family member other than the insured will ensure that the policy and its proceeds are not considered part of your estate. Since life insurance rates change over time and insurers create additional enhancements to policies, it is important to have existing policies reviewed every few years. Oftentimes, an existing policy can be exchanged for a new, less expensive or enhanced policy with no tax effect to the owner of the policy.

- **Consider making annual gifts.** Some smart wealth transfer strategies can be implemented while you are alive, of course. You can make direct gifts to anyone up to a certain amount without incurring a tax bill or eroding your lifetime exemption. This has the potential to reduce the size of your taxable estate in the process.

Wealth and Income Protection

This component of Advanced Planning involves employing strategies to ensure that your wealth is not subjected to claims from potential creditors, litigants, ex-spouses and children's spouses, as well as to protect against catastrophic losses and identity fraud.

It is best to start by evaluating all current insurance policies to determine if you are over- or under-insured for certain coverages, then decide if there are areas of coverage you are missing that need to be addressed. Some types of insurance to consider include:

- **Insurance on your home, car and other assets.** You need enough liability insurance to protect your wealth as well as adequate property insurance for your belongings. You should make sure that your insurance coverage includes all perils applicable to each asset (such as fire, flood, earthquake, hurricane, etc.).

- **Long-term disability insurance.** If a major disability prevented you from working, this insurance would help replace the job-related income you would lose. In particular, younger, high-income earners should consider disability insurance.

- **Long-term care insurance.** The costs associated with an extended nursing home stay or home health care services can decimate wealth quickly. Long-term care insurance is becoming an increasingly important area of coverage, especially as the millions of baby boomers enter into their retirement years.

Business owners might also want to consider strategies to protect their wealth and the value of their businesses. Some options to consider include:

- **Buy-sell agreement.** This is a type of agreement between co-owners of a business that details what happens to the firm if a co-owner dies or leaves the business. Typically funded with life and/or disability insurance, it can help to ensure business continuity and protect the wealth that has been built up in a business over time.

- **Ownership structures.** Various types of trusts and partnerships — such as family limited partnerships — can effectively put assets out of reach of creditors or make it extremely difficult for them to collect money. Likewise, structuring a business as a Limited Liability Company can protect owners and managers from being named in a lawsuit against their company. Even though these ownership structures can limit personal liability, they do not eliminate the need for liability insurance coverage for the entity itself.

Other protection strategies that may be worth considering include:

- **Pre- and post-nuptial agreements.** Some couples, either before or after they are married, choose to enter into a formal, written contract that spells out how property will be divided as well as the terms of spousal support in the event of a divorce. These agreements are especially important to consider when one spouse is significantly wealthier than the other. Each party to the agreement should engage his or her own legal representative in order to avoid conflicts and issues in the future.

- **Identify theft protection strategies.** Effective low-tech actions that can protect you include: reducing the amount of crucial ID and information you carry in your wallet or purse, keeping documents like your Social Security card and passport at home and shredding account statements and financial documents. High-tech solutions include sending financial information only over a guaranteed secure connection, never responding to unsolicited "phisher" emails requesting personal information, installing and updating anti-virus, anti-spam and anti-malware software on your computer and downloading security patches to your computer that can help block intruders. There are also services available that can notify you anytime your credit report has been accessed, allowing you to prevent unauthorized use of your identity for fraudulent purposes.

Charitable Planning

This, of course, involves ways to help you fulfill any philanthropic goals you might have and maximize the effectiveness of your charitable intent — ideally to enable you to make gifts that are significantly greater in value than what would have been able to be made otherwise. Commonly used charitable planning strategies that you should review include:

- **Outright cash gifts.** Direct gifts of cash to qualified charities are deductible for income tax purposes (up to a certain percentage of your adjusted gross income and assuming you itemize and have the proper documentation). Gifts also help to reduce the value of your estate for estate tax purposes.

- **Gifts of appreciated assets.** By donating assets such as stocks that have risen in value directly to a charity, you can generally avoid the capital gains tax you would incur if you sold the asset first and then donated the cash proceeds. This technique is especially valuable for individuals who have large unrealized capital gain positions in specific investments.

- **Donor-advised funds.** Donor-advised funds are pooled investments owned and controlled by a sponsoring organization. You, as the donor, make an irrevocable contribution to the fund and get an immediate tax deduction. The fund invests the money, while allowing you to recommend specific donations, and the donor-advised fund makes the grant. The costs and administrative responsibilities of using such a fund are typically much less than running a private foundation.

- **Charitable trusts.** Several types of trusts allow investors to support favorite charities while generating other benefits. For example, a charitable remainder trust (CRT) enables you to gift assets to the trust. You would receive a tax deduction and avoid paying capital gains taxes on the assets donated. You would then receive income from the trust for a period of years. Once that period of time ends, the remaining amount of assets would go to your chosen charity. Additionally, the assets are removed from your estate for tax purposes.

- **Private foundations.** Charitably-minded investors who are relatively affluent and who want the maximum level of control over their gifting often choose to set up their own private foundation. Private foundations enable donors to control the investment of assets and strategies for grants and gifts. However, private foundations are more expensive than other options and include more rules and regulations (and therefore more administrative duties) than other philanthropic vehicles. Private foundations can be appropriate for families who would like to leave a lasting legacy, enabling future generations to continue a foundation's mission for many years after the passing of the original principals.

Trusted Advisory Relationships: Coordinating *Structured Wealth Management*

Identifying and addressing all of these advanced planning issues is a tall order. It becomes even more challenging when you attempt to coordinate and integrate investment portfolio decisions with wealth transfer, protection and enhancement strategies.

But the fact is, all of your financial decisions should be made by considering all of the other aspects of your specific situation. That's because all of the various components of your financial life are connected, and they must be treated that way in order to make optimal choices. Decisions you make about your investment portfolio or your business, for example, could have a significant impact on your tax situation and eventually your ability to transfer wealth to heirs effectively. Because all of these issues relate to and influence each other, you need to be sure your *Structured Wealth Management* plan takes a truly comprehensive approach.

The good news is that you don't have to do all this by yourself. Because no one person can be an expert in the entire range of *Structured Wealth Management* needs and solutions, you (or your advisor) should instead build relationships with specialists — trusted professionals who have deep knowledge across the range of wealth management specialties and who are well-versed in their particular specialty as it relates to the needs of high-net-worth investors.

A network of Trusted Advisory Relationships is typically composed of at least four core team members:

- A wealth manager
- An estate planning attorney
- A certified public accountant
- An insurance specialist

The wealth manager should act as the general manager — the one person in charge of defining your goals and key challenges. This role can be filled by a trusted financial advisor, or you can take on the job yourself and serve as your own wealth manager. Regardless, a wealth manager should know enough to be able to recognize when there may be an opportunity to add value in any or all aspects of your financial life — but should always rely on the network of Trusted Advisory Relationships to positively identify those opportunities.

The estate planning attorney will be responsible primarily for estate planning and other related legal needs — critical areas of concern for most investors. Among these issues are the creation of your estate plan, gifting strategies, asset protection, succession planning, business planning for entrepreneurs and philanthropic consulting.

A certified public accountant will spearhead income tax preparation, planning and compliance. He or she will also work closely with the estate planning attorney to manage and minimize tax issues that result from various estate planning initiatives and business planning strategies.

The fourth core member of your team of trusted advisors should be an insurance specialist. He or she will work closely with the other core team members to identify and structure solutions to mitigate or eliminate the various risks you face in your financial life. When it comes to this type of professional, look for an insurance broker rather than an insurance agent. A broker works for you — his or her client — while an agent works for a specific company or companies. In all cases, you want to work with a professional who puts your interests before theirs.

Additionally, there are a number of other experts beyond the four core members that you may need to work with occasionally (or perhaps just once). Say, for example, that you need a credit expert to read and summarize loan documents. Very often you can find the appropriate expert at the community level — for example, through your bank or mortgage lender. Other professionals who you may require on a one-off basis include a derivatives specialist, who deals with concentrated stock positions; a securities lawyer, who supports the work of the derivatives specialist; an actuary, who is often needed to consult on various pension and retirement plan issues; and a valuation specialist, who may be required to appraise your business interests, real estate or collectibles. Keep in mind that this is only a partial list of professionals that may be needed on an ad-hoc basis.

You don't need to have close relationships with every one of these experts. Instead, you should be able to rely on your core team members to bring in their own experts as needed. While you may have direct relationships with some specialists, these relationships should be secondary to your core team.

Exhibit 10-2: **The Range of Trusted Advisory Relationships**

Clearly, tremendous value can be realized by building a comprehensive plan that addresses both investment-related matters and non-investment concerns in a coordinated manner using appropriate experts. That, essentially, is what *Structured Wealth Management* is all about — providing solutions to investors' full range of financial issues and integrating those solutions in a way that enables investors to achieve all that is truly important to them in all areas of their lives.

In the next chapter, we'll pull together everything we've shown you so far about *Structured Wealth Management* so you can incorporate it into your own life and make the best possible choices about your wealth.

The tax information herein is general in nature and should not be considered legal or tax advice. Individuals should consult an attorney or tax advisor for specific information on how tax laws apply to their situation. Laws of a particular state or laws that may be applicable to a particular situation may have an impact on applicability, accuracy or completeness of information contained in this book.

CHAPTER 11

Putting It All Together

At this stage, you know the main components of *Structured Wealth Management*. And you have seen that, unlike traditional approaches to financial planning, it is designed to tie together all the aspects of your financial life — from investments to the advanced planning concerns that are becoming increasingly important to many Americans — and help you manage them in a coordinated way.

As a result, *Structured Wealth Management* enables you to define the most important goals in your life and then position your assets to pursue those goals in a systematic way. This means that your wealth means more than just a number on your balance sheet — it is the vehicle for ensuring that you and your loved ones live the type of meaningful, purpose-driven lives that you dream of.

Now you're ready to begin implementing *Structured Wealth Management* into your own financial life. Before you begin, however, take a moment to review the key steps in the process.

Your Total Investment Profile

The first step toward developing a plan that helps you accomplish what you most want is to determine those people, things and values that are most important to you, the biggest challenges you face, and how you truly desire to live your ideal life.

To accomplish this step, you'll want to develop a Total Investor Profile, which, as detailed in chapter 3, is a comprehensive picture of you and your wealth. This Profile will encompass your key values, goals, relationships, your assets and advisors, and your preferred process for managing your financial life and your interests. Armed with a clear, detailed understanding of those issues, you can set out to create the ideal *Structured Wealth Management* plan for you — one that will serve as a guide so that every financial decision you make supports what you most want.

As you'll remember, the key to developing a Total Investor Profile is to go through what we call the Discovery Process. This systematic, detailed interview process enables you to define your financial needs and goals and compare them to your current financial condition — giving you the information needed to create a comprehensive and accurate profile that will be used to create solutions and work with other advisors who may be involved in the wealth management process.

Create Your Investment Plan

Your investment portfolio and the overall plan that guides it play a crucial role in helping you achieve the growth and capital preservation you need to realize your most meaningful financial goals. The creation of your investment plan should be driven by the following key guidelines:

- **Markets work.** Investors who attempt to beat the market by picking and choosing certain stocks or by jumping in and out of the markets nearly always end up underperforming the overall market. The reason: Capital markets generally work in such an efficient manner that it is extraordinarily difficult to consistently outperform the market. We believe a better approach is to simply attempt to capture the rate of return that the market offers over time — and the way to do that is extreme-broad global diversification.

- **Risk and return are related.** As an investor, it's important to take only those risks that have been shown over time to reward investors consistently. Decades of academic research reveal that there are three factors that are primary drivers of long-term returns:

1. *Market factor.* Market risk is the risk of investing in the equity market as a whole versus investing in a riskless asset. Over time, equities have higher expected returns than bonds on a risk-adjusted basis, although that outperformance comes at the cost of higher volatility than bonds.

2. *Size factor.* Small-company stocks have rewarded investors with significantly higher returns over time than large-company stocks. Small companies, in general, tend to be riskier than large, well-established companies — they may grow to be industry giants, or they might go bankrupt.

3. *Price factor.* So-called value stocks of companies in some form of financial distress are typically riskier than shares of fast-growing, financially healthy growth companies. And just as with small-company stocks, value stocks have generally rewarded investors over time by generating higher returns than growth stocks.

Bottom line: We believe that your investment strategy should center around three major decisions. First, how much money you will allocate to stocks versus to bonds, T-bills and cash. Second, how much of your equity capital you will allocate to value stocks versus growth stocks. And third, how much money you will allocate to small-cap stocks versus large-cap stocks.

- **Diversify with structure.** When it comes to investing, risk cannot be eliminated, but it can potentially be reduced or mitigated through the prudent approach of structured diversification:

  1. **Combine multiple asset classes** that have historically experienced dissimilar return patterns across various financial and economic environments.

2. **Diversify globally** — More than 50% of global stock market value is non-U.S., and international stock markets as a whole have historically experienced dissimilar return patterns to the U.S.

3. **Invest in thousands of securities** to limit portfolio losses by reducing company-specific risk.

4. **Invest in high-quality, short-term fixed income.** Consider shorter maturities that have low correlations historically with stocks. And lower default risk with high-quality instruments.

Structured diversification strengthens your ability to grow and protect your money over time — and offers you the potential to come out at the end of your journey with more wealth than you would have if you didn't diversify.

• **Determine the appropriate portfolio for your specific situation.** The right portfolio for you will take into account your specific goals, time horizon, income and liquidity needs, and your ability and willingness to take on investment risk in pursuit of your objectives. Structuring your portfolio based on these issues will help ensure that your portfolio provides you with the appropriate level of risk and return so that you can stick with your plan during a variety of market cycles in order to reach your financial goals. In addition, your portfolio should be structured to help mitigate the effects of taxes on the accumulation and preservation of your wealth. An example of tax management would be to place investments that generate significant taxable income in tax-deferred accounts.

Create Your Advanced Plan

A formal investment plan, while critically important to a successful financial life, is not the only component of comprehensive *Structured Wealth Management*. True wealth management goes beyond financial and investment planning by creating an Advanced Plan to address key non-investment related issues that the vast majority of us face each day. For example:

- How can you preserve your wealth so that you have the money required to meet your needs and fulfill your goals — not just today, but for decades to come?

- How can you keep more of what you earn and pay less to the taxman?

- How can you use your wealth to help children, grandchildren and other heirs lead successful and meaningful lives — now and after you're gone?

- How can you protect your income and assets from creditors, ex-spouses, a major disability, or huge nursing home or other health care costs?

- What can you do to maximize your support for non-profit organizations and causes that you care about deeply?

The Advanced Planning component of *Structured Wealth Management* is designed with these questions in mind. An effective Advanced Plan will be formulated around the following four areas:

- **Wealth Enhancement.** This is the process of maximizing the tax efficiency of current assets and cash flow as well as minimizing fees and unnecessary costs (while achieving both growth and preservation goals).

- **Wealth Transfer.** This process can ensure that you are able to pass along assets in ways that are the most tax-efficient, that satisfy your wishes and that provide for the financial health and well-being of your family.

- **Wealth and Income Protection.** This involves employing strategies, such as trusts and insurance, to ensure that your wealth is not subjected to claims from potential creditors, litigants, ex-spouses and children's spouses, as well as protecting against catastrophic losses and identity fraud.

- **Charitable Planning.** This, of course, involves ways to help you fulfill any philanthropic goals you might have and maximize the effectiveness of your charitable intent — ideally to enable you to make gifts that are significantly greater in value than what you would have been able to make otherwise.

Invest for the Long Term

Taking a long term approach and exercising patience and discipline with your *Structured Wealth Management* plan are in many ways the most important determinant of your eventual financial success or failure. Making frequent changes to your portfolio, for example, increases the risk of sub-par returns and less wealth over time than if you had made fewer changes. Moving in and out of markets and asset classes may result in investors missing those relatively small number of days when markets soar unexpectedly. It's therefore vital that you stick to your investment and advanced plan — especially during periods when the financial markets are behaving in extreme ways.

Of course, remaining patient and disciplined can be extremely difficult when stocks or other assets are soaring or plummeting. The way our brains are hard-wired can cause us to make emotional decisions about our money at precisely the wrong moments — such as buying hot stocks right before they're about to fall and selling stocks just before they're about to rally — that can damage our financial lives.

The solution is to build safeguards into your *Structured Wealth Management* plan that help you stay focused on the long term and tune out the noise that occurs from day to day. Such safeguards include:

- **An Investment Policy Statement.** An IPS is a written document spelling out the key components of your financial situation and investment plan. During particularly strong or weak market environments, it can serve as a reminder of your reasons for structuring your portfolio the way you have. An IPS can also prevent you from making mistakes such as chasing performance or market timing. Whenever you are tempted to make a change to your investment plan, it's best to consult your IPS and remind yourself of the goals, needs and principles that should be driving your decision-making. If a change you want to make conflicts with your IPS, you'll want to stop and assess if it really makes sense to move forward. If, however, your specific circumstances have actually changed, and your goals and needs are greater or less than they were before, a modification to your plan may make sense. In that case, a revision to the IPS should be made reflecting the change of circumstances and the corresponding change to your plan.

- **A rebalancing discipline.** As financial markets rise and fall, your portfolio's exposure to stocks, bonds, cash and other investments will tend to fluctuate as well. Over time, your overall target asset allocations can shift — leaving you with more money in stocks and less in bonds, for example. By rebalancing your portfolio back to its target allocations, you'll better control the level of risk in your portfolio and give yourself a system for minimizing emotional decision-making.

Get The Help You Need

Building a comprehensive plan that coordinates investment- and portfolio-related needs with advanced planning requires a great deal of effort, expertise and time. Given all the components that *Structured Wealth Management* seeks to tie together and manage seamlessly, it's challenging for any one person — even a trained professional — to do everything alone.

For that reason, it's important to implement your wealth management plan with the help of a network of trusted advisory relationships — experts who have deep knowledge across the entire range of wealth management specialties and who can work together to coordinate all aspects of your financial life. Depending on your individual situation, this network should be composed of four core team members:

- A wealth manager
- An estate planning attorney
- A certified public accountant
- An insurance specialist

Working as a team, these professionals can effectively address the various wealth management issues that today's investors face. The wealth manager should act as the general manager or quarterback — the one person in charge of defining your goals and key challenges and coordinating the efforts of the other team members. This role can be filled by a trusted financial advisor, or you can take on the job yourself by serving as your own wealth manager who will build and oversee your network of expert professionals.

This *Structured Wealth Management* approach is being used by many of today's most successful investors and families to make prudent financial decisions. And while some of those investors choose to implement *Structured Wealth Management* entirely on their own, we find that most prefer to work with a professional wealth manager who is capable of devoting significant expertise and resources to the process. Therefore, in the next chapter, we will discuss the benefits of working with an advisor and offer advice for selecting an advisor who can work in your best interests by implementing *Structured Wealth Management*.

CHAPTER 12

Selecting the Right Advisor

As you seek to implement *Structured Wealth Management*, you have a critical decision to make: Should you try to do it yourself, or should you enlist the assistance of a financial advisor?

This decision will come down to a number of factors — such as the level of expertise you possess in the various areas of investment planning and advanced planning that *Structured Wealth Management* addresses, as well as the amount of time you can dedicate to creating and maintaining a comprehensive plan. You'll also need to consider whether you want to spend your free time personally dealing with the full range of financial challenges and opportunities you face, or if you would prefer to devote that time to family, hobbies and other pursuits that give your life purpose and meaning.

Although some investors choose to manage their financial lives entirely by themselves, we have noticed that in recent years, many investors have increasingly looked to professional financial advisors for guidance. Additionally, as individual investors' wealth increases, so does their tendency to delegate the oversight of their financial life to a financial advisor.

Make no mistake: Choosing a financial advisor is one of the most important decisions you may ever make. There are an enormous number of financial professionals out there who want to work with you. However, far too few offer the type of comprehensive, consultative approach that we have outlined in this book. If you believe that

Structured Wealth Management will help you make the smartest possible decisions about your money, then you absolutely need to work with someone who agrees with your belief and has adopted this approach.

Should You Work With An Advisor?

The challenges that have occurred in the financial markets during the past decade have prompted many investors to seek professional help managing their investments as well as other areas of their financial lives.

An experienced advisor can provide a number of benefits, including:

- **Expertise.** We've all been reminded repeatedly in recent years that navigating financial markets is not an easy task. Additionally, the intricacies of wealth management — building a plan that takes into account investments, estate planning, tax strategies, wealth preservation and other components — can make coordinating your financial life a difficult job. The role of a good advisor is to understand the crucial needs and goals of clients and then assemble the requisite expertise to address those needs and reach those goals. That expertise should ideally come from both the advisor and a team of trusted experts with whom the advisor works and closely coordinates, to help solve clients' concerns.

- **Discipline.** As you've learned, investors are often their own worst enemies — buying high, selling low and putting their financial futures in jeopardy. A professional advisor should have the knowledge, experience and objectivity to "take a step back" during volatile market environments, prevent investors from making bad or emotional decisions about their finances in the heat of the moment, and help them stay true to their long-term course.

- **Time.** An advisor's job is to focus on helping you at every step so that you don't have to do all the work — leaving you with more time to spend with family, on leisure activities or maximizing your current income and earnings potential. Of course, some investors enjoy spending much of their free time working on their investments and even their financial plans. And while that's certainly not a bad way to spend your time, we find that most investors prefer to pursue other interests beyond wealth management when they have the opportunity to do so.

- **Perspective.** Advisors work with many clients who share similar financial concerns and issues. Over time this can help advisors gain valuable perspectives about how to solve problems and capture opportunities in the most effective and creative way. By contrast, investors working on their own are largely limited to their individual experiences when trying to confront complex financial issues.

Of course, in some instances, a professional advisor may not be necessary. If, for example, you have a modest amount of assets and your financial situation is extremely straightforward and easy for you to fully comprehend, you may not require the expertise that an advisor brings. In that case, you may be well served by building a well-diversified portfolio of low-cost mutual funds and periodically reviewing and rebalancing your asset allocation to stay on course.

If your situation is more complex, however, an advisor may be able to add substantial value. If, for example, you have significant wealth, children and other heirs you wish to take care of, an ex-spouse (or two), and a child with special needs, it makes sense to consider working with an advisor.

To help you decide if an advisor is a good option, consider the following questions:

- Are you in a position to spend a significant amount of time each day and week managing your financial life? If so, do you want to spend your free time in that way — or are there other interests you would rather pursue?

- What is your level of expertise about investments, tax management strategies, estate planning techniques, wealth protection options, charitable gifting tools and other key components of an investment plan and an advanced plan?

- How willing are you to stay up-to-date with changes in the tax code, estate planning laws and other developments that could affect your plan and financial future?

- How confident are you in your ability to consistently make the smartest possible decisions about your financial life, year after year, in all the areas that affect you and are important to you and your family?

What to Look for in a Financial Advisor

Any financial advisor you work with should be willing and able to bring significant value to your financial life. Unfortunately, too many advisors today do not offer much in the way of value and don't always put their clients' best interests ahead of theirs. Instead of working to coordinate your financial life and solve your biggest concerns, many are more focused on selling you products and earning commissions, regardless of whether those products are the best fit for your needs and situation.

The upshot: Not any financial advisor will do. You need to work only with those advisors who will implement strategies that will maximize your chances of achieving your goals. If you don't currently work with an advisor, that means you must locate and identify ideal advisors for your needs. If you do currently work with an advisor, you need to evaluate him or her carefully and ask yourself if you are truly receiving the benefits and value that you want, need and deserve.

Whatever you do, don't settle for mediocrity. If you're not sure that you can implement *Structured Wealth Management* on your own, get help from the right advisor. If your current advisor isn't aligned with the philosophy and principles of *Structured Wealth Management*, consider working with an advisor who uses this approach with clients.

We have worked with hundreds of advisors over the years and have seen the factors that differentiate successful, client-focused advisors from the rest of the pack. As you evaluate advisors to work with, ask the following questions:

- **What are the advisor's designations and experience?** Advisors' professional designations can tell you a lot about them. The single most important designation to look for when evaluating an advisor is whether or not he or she is an independent advisor. Independent advisors are legally required to act as a fiduciary — which means they must always look out for your best interests as the client and disclose all important information to you, including fees charged and any conflicts of interest. In short, it is illegal for them to engage in any situation that would serve their interests over yours.

  In addition, ask if the advisor has an advanced designation such as Certified Financial Planner™. A CFP® designation tells you that the advisor has received formal education and training on a wide variety of financial planning topics and has passed an exam testing their financial planning knowledge and skills. CFPs also are required to take continuing education courses each year to stay current on financial planning-related issues. If the advisor is not a CFP, inquire about how many years he or she has been in the financial services industry. With non-CFPs, you'd like to see that they have at least five years' experience (and preferably more).

  Here's one title you should not automatically pay much attention to: Wealth Manager. Today, lots of advisors have taken to calling themselves "wealth managers." And while some are — such as those who follow the types of processes outlined in this book — others are wealth managers in name only who don't offer anything beyond investment basics. So don't assume that a so-called wealth manager practices *Structured Wealth Management*. Instead, dig deeper.

- **What is the advisor's fees and compensation structure?** An advisor's fee structure can tell you a great deal about what your experience working together may be like. For example, a fee-based advisor usually charges a percentage of your portfolio's assets each year. That means the advisor does well only if he helps you grow and protect your wealth and gets you closer to your goals. If his decisions cause you to lose wealth, he earns less. The upshot: A fee-based advisor has a legal, moral and economic incentive to give you the best advice about your wealth. If, for example, the smartest thing to do at a particular moment is to stay disciplined and maintain your current asset allocation, that's exactly what a good fee-based advisor should recommend. Many investors are also increasingly choosing to work with fee-only advisors. As the name suggests, these advisors are compensated only through fees rather than commissions, which are generated based on trading activity.

  By contrast, a commission-based advisor usually gets paid only when he buys or sells an investment for your portfolio. He may try to work in your best interests, but at the same time, he has a powerful incentive to trade your stocks frequently or move in and out of asset classes often in order to generate a higher income for himself. Regardless of whether your wealth rises or falls, the commission-based broker still gets paid. Clearly this presents a strong potential for a conflict of interests — which is why we believe it is best that you work only with fee-based advisors.

- **What types of clients does the advisor serve?** Many top fee-based independent advisors have a clearly defined type of client they serve. It might be broad-based (retirees, for example) or highly-focused (such as executives in the health care profession). This targeted approach offers two advantages. For one, it means they have specific knowledge and expertise to serve their clients effectively and solve their biggest issues. It also means that if you are not a good fit for a particular advisor you are evaluating, the advisor should tell you so and recommend another advisor who would be a better option. The advisor won't take you on as a client simply to bring in more revenue for herself.

- **Is the advisor consultative?** You also want to work only with a consultative advisor — that is, one who works hard to understand your specific, unique goals and needs and then works in partnership with you and other professionals to create a customized wealth management plan designed around those goals and needs. In short, a consultative advisor is acutely focused on solving your problems.

Perhaps the clearest sign of whether an advisor is consultative or not will occur the first time you meet. A consultative advisor will let you do plenty of talking about what you are looking for, and will ask you questions designed to identify what is really important to you and your family. The best consultative advisors will even have a formal method for uncovering those issues, such as the discovery process that we have highlighted in this book.

By contrast, a non-consultative advisor will most likely spend much of your first meeting talking at you — perhaps telling you how impressive his performance record is, how big his staff is, or listing all the impressive products he can offer you. This might sound good on the surface. But remember: An advisor's job is to do all he or she can to help you reach your most important goals so you can lead a meaningful and happy life. If you encounter an advisor who takes little interest in those issues from the start — or asks you just a handful of basic, cursory questions about you and your concerns — chances are the advisor is most interested in getting just enough information from you to recommend a specific product. He's probably not too concerned about helping you coordinate your entire financial life. In such cases, you should look elsewhere for help.

Another good indication that the advisor is consultative is if she uses a defined process for meeting with clients and helping them on a regular basis. In Chapter 3, for example, we outlined the *Structured Wealth Management* process, which consists of a series of five scheduled meetings between advisor and client. These five meetings ensure that your plan starts out on the right foot and stays that way year after year. Therefore, when you meet with an advisor, make sure to ask her to spell out her approach for working with clients on a regular basis, and decide if her answers indicate a consultative approach with regular meetings.

- **Does the advisor sell performance?** When an advisor you interview discusses his investment methodology, pay close attention. Does she highlight how much he's beaten the market lately or emphasize her ability to generate huge returns through a "specialized" or "proprietary" approach? If so, be wary. The promise of consistent market-beating returns (or suggestions along those lines) is a big red flag. As you'll remember, decades of research show that accurately predicting the winning and losing investments, asset classes and markets year after year is hugely difficult — nearly impossible, really. An advisor who sells performance as the primary reason to work with him is really just a salesman who is likely to continually buy and sell products in your portfolio — and rack up big commissions in the process, even if he fails to deliver that promised outperformance.

  We've witnessed more of this performance-selling in recent years as the markets have been increasingly volatile. Many advisors today like to talk about the ability to offer "downside protection" and "advanced" techniques that will get clients in and out of the markets at just the right times. We think this is simply market timing disguised as risk management. Using these approaches, you may win — but the greater likelihood is that you will lose. Regardless, it's a huge gamble to take with your financial future.

  If you believe (as we do) that the most prudent investment approach is to try and capture market rates of return, then it clearly makes sense to work with an advisor who is aligned with your thinking and investment philosophy.

- **Does the advisor bring specific expertise to solve your biggest concerns?** As we've noted before, the full range of your wealth management concerns are diverse and complex. To effectively understand and solve them in an integrated and holistic manner, an advisor needs to bring expertise and skilled resources to the process. In rare cases, an advisor may possess all the skills needed to build and maintain a well-crafted *Structured Wealth Management* plan. Typically, however, you'll want to see that an advisor has access to the expertise you require and can coordinate the efforts of a team of trusted professionals — which should typically include a CPA, an estate planning attorney and an insurance specialist — to create ideal, holistic solutions. These professionals can either be located in-house at the advisor's firm or they can be outside of the advisory firm. Either way, you want to be sure you are working with someone who can provide the specific expertise needed to address the crucial issues you face.

- **What tools does the advisor use to maintain your wealth management plan?** Think about all the "moving parts" of a *Structured Wealth Management* plan that we have discussed in this book. Clearly, such a plan cannot be created and put in a drawer. It needs to be monitored, reviewed and updated on occasion. That's why you need to know what tools and criteria an advisor uses to maintain clients' plans and keep them current.

  Here you want to see that the advisor has invested in and uses advanced technology such as financial planning software. You will also want to see that the advisor has a systematic, disciplined method for reviewing clients' objectives and risk tolerance, and rebalancing portfolios to realign asset allocations in ways that are tax efficient. Finally, ask if the advisor creates an Investment Policy Statement for each client. As mentioned earlier, an IPS should detail all the key components of your investment plan. Because of its ability to help keep investors on track and mindful of their choices, we believe an IPS is absolutely crucial to a successful plan.

- **Do you trust the advisor?** A great advisor is someone who you — and probably your spouse or partner and other family members

— will work with for decades. But for that to happen, you need to respect and trust the advisor and feel comfortable working with her. An advisor may score well on all the other questions above, but if you two don't "click," the relationship may be less productive and enjoyable than it should be. Once you've met with an advisor a few times, ask yourself if you think she is the type of person who will always have your best interests in mind, who you will want to work with on a regular basis, and who you would refer friends and family to. Then, ask for referrals — and contact them to discuss their opinions of the advisor and their experiences with her.

Finally, look for signs that the advisor is not "the next Bernie Madoff" who will rip you off. Some safeguards include: custodying your assets at an outside firm and not in-house at the advisor's firm; using highly-regulated products such as mutual funds; and ensuring that the firm holding your assets has Securities Investor Protection Corporation (SIPC) insurance, which should protect your wealth in the event of advisor fraud. Also, remember the old adage "if it sounds too good to be true, it probably is." If an advisor makes wild claims — she can deliver positive returns in any environment or can generate 10% a year no matter what — walk out the door.

- **Does the advisor have a clean record?** In addition, you can research an advisor's background to see if he's ever been censured or received client complaints by going to the BrokerCheck feature on the Financial Industry Regulatory Authority's website (www.finra. org/Investors/ToolsCalculators/BrokerCheck). This site only covers advisors who work with a broker dealer. For independent advisors, go to the Investment Adviser Public Disclosure website (IAPD) at www.adviserinfo.sec.gov. If an advisor has any prior complaints or enforcement actions on his record, go back and ask the advisor for details about the situation and decide after that if you should consider working with him or her. For some investors with substantial wealth, having a background check run on a potential advisor can ensure that the advisor has not run afoul of financial regulatory agencies in the past, or has not been convicted of certain crimes.

The Next Step Is Yours

Whether you work with a financial advisor or go it alone, we firmly believe that the single most important move you can make today is to start implementing *Structured Wealth Management* into your own financial life.

Now that you've read this book, take a minute to think again about your most important goals — the things you truly value on a deep and personal level, and the things you most want and need to achieve in order to live a comfortable, meaningful and satisfied life. Then think about all the important people in your life- your spouse or partner, your children or your parents — and the hopes and dreams you have for them, as well as any challenges that they face. Finally, consider any causes or issues that you care about and want to support — which might include anything from fighting global poverty to supporting your city's symphony orchestra.

When you think about all of these components, one fact is illuminated: You and your wealth can do an enormous amount of good for many, many people in your family, your community and the world at large. Even if you never become a millionaire or consider yourself wealthy, you can still have a huge impact and positively shape your life and the lives of others. What a fantastic position to be in! In the end, then, you have a responsibility to make smart decisions about your wealth so that it can do as much good as possible. You owe it to yourself and to the people and organizations you care about most to do the job right.

Ultimately, this is where *Structured Wealth Management* can make all the difference. The *Structured Wealth Management* process was designed with one overarching goal in mind: To enable you to coordinate and comprehensively manage all the key parts of your financial life, no matter how complex, so that you can solve your biggest financial challenges and achieve everything that is important to you.

Over our decades of experience in financial services, we've seen a lot of ideas and approaches come and go. But in all that time, we have never seen a better, smarter or more effective way for investors to manage their wealth than *Structured Wealth Management.* Its consultative process from which customized solutions are designed and coordinated by a team of experts to work seamlessly together has helped many of today's most successful families get exactly what they want out of life.

The next step is yours. You have an opportunity to achieve a higher level of financial success than you may have thought possible, and have a higher level of confidence that your goals and aspirations will come to fruition. Seize this opportunity now to create benefits for yourself and those around you that could resonate for generations to come.

We wish you a lifetime of financial and personal success.

How to Lose Money

Harry M. Markowitz, PhD

1990 Nobel Prize Laureate in Economic Sciences and Member, Loring Ward Investment Committee

If you want to become an acknowledged Saint, it is best if you start by giving away all your money. If this prospect sounds too daunting, the following are four efficient suggestions for reducing your wealth. The first two may only lose most of it but the final two will make it all disappear.

The first advice toward achieving poverty on your way to Sainthood is to invest in the hottest stocks in the hottest sector: Buy auto stocks when the car is the latest new invention; purchase tech stocks when they are the "in" thing; invest in mortgage-based derivatives when all the "smart" money is doing the same. Under no circumstances should you read Charles Mackay's book *Extraordinary Popular Delusions and the Madness of Crowds*. Instead, just try your utmost to keep up with the thundering herd.

If you are too cautious to follow the preceding advice, here is some rock-solid, very sensible, traditional advice: Put all your money in some big, trusted company — like the one you work for, the one that already pays your salary — like Eastern Airlines, Penn Central, or Enron.

The aforementioned ways of losing money involve buying stocks traded on exchanges, such as the NYSE and NASDAQ. But if you do not want to invest in these, because you don't trust the guy on TV who barks advice at you, listen to your trusted neighbor or uncle who knows a brilliant investor who has figured out how to double your money in less than a year! I know of a guy like that: His name was Charles Ponzi.

Last, but not least, find a financial advisor who will take care of your money for you. To be sure to lose money and perfect your plan for poverty, do not work with an advisor such as recommended in this book. Instead, find an advisor who provides the added service of holding your money for you rather than having you keep it with a large, nationally recognized custodian that periodically sends, directly to you, reports of how your account is doing.

More generally, for optimal effect, just ignore the advice in this book.

ABOUT THE AUTHORS

Alex Potts

President and Chief Executive Officer, Loring Ward

Alex Potts is the President and C.E.O. of Loring Ward Group Inc. and its affiliates, as well as the SA Funds – Investment Trust.

Potts founded and was President, Chief Executive Officer and Director of Loring Ward Securities Inc. (formerly Assante Capital Management Inc.). In addition, he served as Executive Vice President and General Manager of LWI Financial Inc. (formerly Assante Asset Management, Inc.). In 1999, Alex started the SA Funds – Investment Trust and was named President and Chief Executive Officer.

From 1990 – 2000, he served in various positions at Loring Ward and its predecessor firms, including Senior Vice President of Investment Operation.

Potts earned a Bachelor of Science Degree in Economics from Santa Clara University. He also holds General Securities (Series 7), State Law (Series 63) and General Securities Principal (Series 24) licenses.

Joni L. Clark, CFA, CFP®

Chief Investment Officer, Loring Ward

Joni L. Clark has advised clients on all aspects of investment strategy and portfolio risk management for two decades. Her clients have included affluent individuals and families, investment management organizations and large institutional pension funds.

As Chief Investment Officer of Loring Ward, she directs investment policy and portfolio management strategies for the company. She also chairs the company's Investment Committee.

Prior to joining Loring Ward in 2002, Clark held senior positions with some the country's most respected financial services firms. She began her career at Merrill Lynch PFS (1989-1991). She then worked as Vice President of Wilshire Associates (1991-1998), consulting for large public and corporate defined benefit plans, foundations and endowments, and institutional investment management firms. She also was a Managing Director at Legg Mason Institutional Advisors (1998-2000), overseeing client service for institutional client relationships. And she was a Senior Investment Consultant and Portfolio Manager at Enright Financial Consultants (2000-2002), a boutique investment management firm serving affluent individuals and families.

Clark received a Bachelor of Science degree in Finance in 1988, a Chartered Financial Analyst (CFA) designation in 1994, and became a Certified Financial Planner (CFP®) in 2004. She is a member of the CFA Institute, the Los Angeles Society of Financial Analysts, and the Financial Planning Association.

Eric Golberg, CFP®

Director of Wealth Management, Loring Ward

Eric Golberg is Loring Ward's Director of Wealth Management, responsible for providing Advisors with the tools, resources and services to meet the wealth management needs of their high-net worth clients.

Golberg has spent over 20 years working with high-net worth individuals and families, primarily in the entertainment industry. Most recently, he was in charge of Private Wealth Services at Bellatore, LLC. Previously, he spent 10 years at Nigro, Karlin, Segal & Feldstein, LLP, one of the largest and most prestigious multi-family offices in the nation, handling the financial affairs of numerous executives, entertainers, athletes and musicians. Prior to that, he was a private banker at Union Bank of California, Chase Manhattan, and City National Bank, also working primarily with high-net worth individuals, focusing primarily on financing strategies and investment analysis.

Golberg is a CFP® professional and a member of the Financial Planning Association. He graduated from Southern Utah University with a B.A. in Business Administration.

Steven J. Atkinson, CFS

Executive Vice President, Advisor Relations, Loring Ward

For more than fifteen years, Steve Atkinson has been dedicated to helping create a better experience for independent financial advisors so that they can create a world-class experience for their clients.

As an Executive Vice President at Loring Ward, Atkinson speaks frequently at client and advisor events and has personally coached over 100 advisors.

He is a graduate of the University of Nebraska at Omaha, with a Bachelor of Science degree in Finance and Investment Banking. He is also a Certified Fund Specialist (CFS).

ACKNOWLEDGEMENTS

It took the ideas, hard work and inspiration of many people to create this book. We especially want to thank Mark Klimek and William Chettle for all their help in writing, editing and organizing our thoughts. Thank you to Susy McInerny for her careful editing and proofing, Matt Carvalho and Cherry Phan provided the charts and data. Ed Robertson brought his creative talents to the layout and cover design. Chris Stanley, Diana Dorn and Elizabeth Cordova provided legal and regulatory guidance. And thanks above all to all our colleagues at Loring Ward for their support and encouragement.